# The Author Online

A Short Guide
to Building Your Website,
Whether You Do it Yourself
(and you can!)
or You Work With Pros

Annik LaFarge

By Annik La Farge
Copyright ©2010 by Title TK Projects LLC, New York, NY

Published by Title TK Projects, New York, NY
ISBN: 978-0-615-37391-1
Book design by Daniel Rembert

Manufactured in the United States of America
First printing: June 2010

Title TK Projects, LLC
P.O. Box 156
Germantown, NY 12534

While the author has made every effort to provide accurate Internet addresses at the time of publication, the author assumes no responsibility for errors, or for changes that occur after publication. Neither the author nor the publisher shall be liable for damages arising herefrom. The fact that an organization or website is referred to in this work as a citation and/or a potential source of further information does not mean that the author endorses the information the organization or website may provide or recommendations it may make.

# Table of Contents

# CHAPTER ONE

# Going Online

**It's a question that every author has to ask:**
*do I need a website?*

For most, the answer is a resounding Yes, but that leads only to a barrage of more difficult questions: What sort of website do I need? What elements should it have? How can I use it to promote both my upcoming book and my backlist? How much of a time commitment must I make to updating the content and adding new material? How can I make it an organic entity that will keep expanding along with my career? And how in the world do I do it?

This short book is intended to answer those questions and more, and serve as your guide to getting started, whether you're working with a designer or building it yourself. This is not a technical manual (it contains one single, solitary, piece of technical instruction), nor is it a marketing primer that aims to tell you how to make your website a success through strategies like search engine optimization and creating keyword-rich page descriptions. There are many good books and articles about those subjects (and I've included a brief list with links in the Resources section). Instead, this book is designed to start at the very beginning of the process: to guide you as you think through and craft a vision of what makes sense for *you,* and your very particular, unique body of work, on the Internet. What I hope you'll find here is the Big Think, both a philosophical and a practical approach.

But before I get started I want you to stop for a moment after that first question – *do I need a website?* – and honestly wrestle with it. I'm not going to try to talk you out of it – if you've gotten this far you probably *do* need a website – but I want you to play devil's advocate with yourself because in doing so you will begin that all-important process of framing your vision for how you want to develop your presence on the web. There are many ways of "being" on the web that don't involve a website, from social networking to blogging on an existing website platform like Blogger or Wordpress. So asking yourself two simple questions at the outset – *do I need a website?* and, *if so, why?* – will serve the valuable purpose of focusing your mind.

Let's begin with the reasons why you might not want to expend the valuable resources of time, energy, and money on a website.

*You are humbled and daunted by the numbers, which suggest you'll end up a lost soul in the wilderness.* According to Bowker, the country's leading provider of bibliographic information, there were 288,355 new books published in 2009 by traditional publishers in the U.S. and 764,448 by self-publishers and micro-niche publishers, for a total of more than a million books. (The latter number includes a huge quantity of previously published books that are now in the public domain.) The number of traditionally published books actually fell a bit. But overall the number of books released during 2009 rose a staggering 87%. According to Netcraft, an Internet monitoring company that has tracked web growth since 1995 (when there were just 18,000 websites with domain names and content on them), in 2009 there were 215,675,903.

Surely you know how hard it is to attract attention to a new book (which is part of the reason you need a website). Looking at these numbers you have to ask yourself: isn't it likely to be even harder to attract attention to a website? I think the answer is conditionally yes, with caveats that relate to how smart you are about building and using your website. That's what this book promises to help you with. So the numbers shouldn't deter you; instead, they should sober you right up and get you more focused.

*The online landscape seems to change every six months and you wonder how you'll ever keep up.* As I write this book (in Spring 2010) the last major writing trend, traditional blogging, has given way to microblogging, in the form of Twitter and Facebook. Facebook alone has more than 400 million users and is competing with Google for the amount of traffic it sends to major portals like Yahoo and MSN. And the way that we read books is undergoing a sea change as new electronic devices that enable reading e-books begin to proliferate and gain in popularity. Even before Apple released its iPad and iBookstore it was reported (by the mobile device advertising agency Mobclix), that the number of e-book apps (27,000) in Apple's iTunes App Store had surpassed the number of games (25,400). Barnes & Noble has the Nook; Sony continues to improve its Reader; and Amazon has a free app that lets anyone access its Kindle storefront without owning the expensive device. Other devices – tablets, netbooks, souped-up mobile phones and who knows what else – are on the horizon and they too will alter the way we connect to content on the web. Less than a year after this book comes out I'll have to revise this paragraph to account for a new wave of developments and innovations. So: as the world of technology constantly changes and evolves, how can an individual author stay relevant and up-to-date on the web?

*You are a writer, not a webmaster.* How are you going to manage to write and promote books – with all the dedication of time and energy that those two enterprises require – and keep a website fresh and interesting? And if it's not fresh and interesting – meaning constantly updated with new material – won't people bounce right off it?

These are all important questions but they have a deceptively simple and common-sense answer. Your grandmother would give you the same advice that I will: *Be prepared. Be adaptable. Be authentic.* I believe – and my experience bolsters that belief – that achieving success on the web has as much to do with careful, focused, honest thinking and a mindful, step-by-step approach, as anything else. It's a process I aim to help you with in the pages that follow, in the tradition of a good, old-fashioned editor.

If you're contemplating a website you may find yourself in one of the following scenarios.

*You have a new book coming out in a few months and you need to be on the web.* Perhaps you don't have a lot of resources of time, energy, or money; you just want to get something up that will properly represent the book and enable people to find you on the Internet. Maybe you're an author who has published books before and you never quite got around to creating a website. Or perhaps you didn't feel you needed one, you didn't understand what it could do for you, or it was so long ago when the last book came out that you were still using a typewriter. Or maybe you're a young journalist and this is your first book; you want to do everything you can to give it a shot, and you want to enable and amplify the efforts of your publicist as much as possible. Or maybe you're self-publishing your book and don't have the benefit of a publisher's muscle in the marketplace; you want to do everything you can to give the book its best chance at success.

*You've published several books, were early on the web and created a site that, at the time, worked very well for you.*

But that was years ago, and your publisher/freelance webmaster still controls everything – you can't make a single change on the site without contacting him. Now your publicist/webmaster has moved on to other things and frankly he's not terribly responsive. You want to basically replicate what you already have – not reinvent the wheel with bells and whistles – and then be able to control all the content you post and develop some new features that might enable you to attract new visitors. You want to begin again, but this time with the ability to use the website as a tool that enables you to do many things, from publishing new material to creating a community and connecting with your fans.

*You've dipped your toe into the online world – created a Facebook page, started Tweeting – and now you want to organize your efforts and be more strategic.* A website or blog is one place where you can bring all your online activities together, and once you've attracted someone's attention through a status update or a Tweet you can bring that person to your home on the web where she can discover your latest book.

## Author.com

My first goal in this book is to get you to think like the author of your website. Instead of regarding it as a "web project" that puts you way outside your comfort zone, put your author hat back on and approach it as you would a fairly complex and detailed book proposal. What you need to do is summon all the deliberation, care and planning that you bring to your writing – and your outlining, positioning, drafting, editing, re-writing – to the project that is your website. The good news is that creating a website is a lot easier and faster than writing a book, and it gets easier every year as new technologies develop to enable even the most ardent of Luddites. You simply have to draw on the same skills that you've developed as an author, and you need to ask yourself many of the same questions at each critical step along the way.

I speak to writers every day about their websites and I always ask the same questions I posed above (and many others that will follow in the pages of this book). I'm always surprised at how liberating and enlightening they find the process of thinking about a website in the same basic way they would think about structuring a book or creating a proposal – something they *do* know how to do. So forget about the fact that the web is a technology you can't possibly understand and think of it instead as a platform for distributing your ideas – like a book – and reaching your audience – like a good publicity and marketing campaign. Once you do that, you'll realize how much you already know about how to do this.

I've spent a lot of years building websites, but at heart I consider myself an editor. I started my publishing career in publicity (at Random House), and as I evolved into an editor I did so with one part of my brain devoted to the enterprise of positioning and "selling" an idea, and the rest dedicated to the finer arts of narrative, expression, and development – the stuff I learned as an English major in college. In this manual I'm going to lead you through the process of thinking through your website by starting at the very beginning: with the content. If you start there and always pay homage to its importance and preeminence, you're going to do yourself proud. I try to avoid clichés in my writing, and urge my authors to do the same. But indulge me here.

Content is king.

*Long live the King.*

## Do it *Myself?*

A word about this before we dive in, which is intended to embolden you. Over the past few years it has become extremely easy to create and maintain a website or a blog. There are many excellent options out there, from traditional website-building tools like Sandvox, a program I've used myself and admire greatly (it's available only on the Mac and comes with blogging features built-in), to pure blogging platforms like Wordpress and Blogger, which enable a non-technical person to create a blog or (by turning off the comments section) a blog-that-looks-like-a-website.

If you're an offline do-it-yourselfer you'll know what it means to imagine what the world was like before there were retailers like Home Depot, Lowe's, or the Garrett Wade tool company; television networks like HGTV and programs like "This Old House"; and publishers of high-quality how-to books like the Taunton Press, Sunset and Reader's Digest. All those companies created accessible and affordable pathways for non-professional people to build things themselves – to take control of an essential part of their domestic lives – and in so doing they changed the way many of us inhabit our world and they unleashed waves of untapped potential and creativity.

Today the Internet abounds with similar opportunity for people who want to create their own online presence, whether through microblogging (Twitter, Facebook), creating a traditional blog or website (Sandvox, Wordpress), or self-publishing and marketing their own book (Lulu.com, CreateSpace,.com, Blurb.com). Or doing all three. The tools and programs to get you started – and evolve into a master, if you're so inclined – are easy-to-use and widely available.

Alongside that explosion of opportunity has come another essential development: the proliferation of information that a layperson can easily access, understand, and use to create, refine, and expand his online world. And because much of the technology and programming for building websites evolved out of the open source movement, much of what you need to get started is free. Moreover, it's constantly updated by professional developers who are motivated by a passion to continually improve the web and enable all of us to use it in new and more creative ways. Often the changes and refinements come from comments or complaints made by regular users on message boards and in user forums – people like you and me. It's a constantly evolving, constantly improving landscape.

In my business I almost always work with a developer because I'm completely non-technical and on most of our projects we do fairly complicated stuff, like running stock portfolios or accepting credit cards. But if I *wanted* to do it myself the fact is that I could, because all the tools, information and tech support are out there, waiting for me to come calling. Even more, it's affordable to practically anyone who owns a computer, and a great deal of it is free. All you have to do is

Google it and chances are you'll find a wealth of simple instructions and often step-by-step videos. [See the Resources section for some websites and businesses that I love and recommend. That list is constantly updated on this book's companion website, TheAuthorOnline.com, where you'll find additional tips and resources about author websites.]

I decided to write this book because not a week goes by that I don't hear from an author, editor, or literary agent with the request for help and advice about building a website. It turns out that most authors – and indeed most agents and editors – simply don't know where to begin. So I thought: why not download everything I know into one short book and keep updating it as time goes by. Then I can help *everyone,* a goal I've nurtured in true Panglossian form since I was a teenager. Also: it became clear to me that many of the people who were calling me needed something quite simple: either an online presence to support a new book that was just coming out or a very basic "home" on the Internet where they could present – in one place and in their own voice – all the information about themselves and their work that they wished to. They didn't need a project manager and in many cases they didn't even need a design or programming partner. With the right kind of guidance they could do it themselves. What most authors need is help deciphering the road ahead, and a way to frame the larger conversation about who they want to be on the web and how to get there.

Building a website yourself is also, I daresay, *fun.* I was speaking to an author friend whom I greatly admire, Amy Krouse Rosenthal (more about her web projects in Chapter

Two) and she told me a story about how her mother gave her "a fun box" when she was a kid. It was filled with magic markers, a ruler, different colored pencils, an eraser, and a nice stack of heavy paper. She would spend hours making and drawing things. Today, as someone active online, she thinks of the web as one giant fun box, filled with tools that will let anyone who has a bit of patience, curiosity, and determination, create a place for themselves on the Internet. An example of a tool she found and made creative use of is Time Toast, a free plug-in that lets you create and share timelines. With this simple tool she was able to represent the narrative of her film, "The Beckoning of Lovely" – which was a community effort that involved hundreds of strangers from around the world – in another dimension, going beyond the simple video clip.

Another benefit to doing it yourself is that once you've built a website you quickly realize that a whole new world is waiting for you – one that's filled with data and information. Harnessing and taking advantage of the tools that deliver all those rich data is just as achievable to you as building the website was. For example, once you get your site launched you can start using – for free – Google's powerful Analytics program that will give you invaluable information about who is coming to your website; where they're coming from; what content they read; how much time they spend on each article; what part of the country or the world (down to the city and state) they come from; and much, much, more.  Why is this useful? Say you're a self-published author and you're planning to load up a few cartons of books in your van and hit the road on your own publicity tour. If you've had a website or a blog that's gotten some traffic over a meaningful period of time you can drill down in Google Analytics to find out which cities in the country send your website the most traffic. So when it comes time to making the decision, Topeka vs. Phoenix, you can let the data inform you. If you have a publicist working with you she can use your data to guide her priorities in terms of pitching local radio stations and other outlets.

You can also use Google's AdWords program to promote your site and its AdSense program to accept ads from businesses and make some money. (More on taking advantage of these programs in Chapter Four.) Email service providers – companies like MailChimp and Constant Contact that manage e-newsletters for individuals as well as large companies – have similar analytics programs that allow you to mine data about who is reading your e-letters; where they live; which links yield the most clicks; how you are doing compared to others in your industry category (investing, health, parenting, entertainment) and more.

Once you start using these services you may be awed, as I was, by the high quality and quantity of Help documentation that these companies provide about how to use their products and, most important, how to make them work for you. Message boards and forums are another great source of information for problem-solving and finding new features you can plug into your website or blog. These, like the open source movement, grew out of a powerful impulse that drove many developers and early Internet pioneers to collaborate on web projects and improve programs, systems and tools for everyone.

I find it both comforting and energizing to know that there's this gigantic safety net of help and information that's waiting to catch me once I slip. And slip I do, all the time. Smart technology companies, whether big ones like Google, GoDaddy and Apple or small ones like Karelia, the maker of Sandvox, have top-flight support departments that can offer additional help if the documentation on the web doesn't suffice. So even though you may spend most of your time writing in your garret with your dog at your feet, you are not alone.

So the first thing you should feel as you wrestle with the question of whether you need a website – and whether you have the energy to build one yourself – is a sense of relief that once you make the decision to go ahead it's actually quite doable, even if you are over twenty five years old. No matter how much of a Luddite you are, if you're capable of writing a book you're also capable of building a useful, functional, elegant, platform for yourself on the web, and you can do it quickly and for very little money. (A Wordpress template, for example, costs as little as $25, though there are dozens of free ones available, as there are on Blogger.)

You do, of course, have to *want* to build a website, and you have to make a deal with yourself to be patient and expect some frustration. But the tools are out there, and with a bit of study and trial-and-error, they are pretty easy to master. What this means is that you can start small and simple, and then grow slowly with feedback from visitors and new technology developments that will enable you to do more and more. That's a new thing for authors, and it's worth getting excited about.

## The Question of Design

Now, you may feel that without a professional designer it's crazy to venture into this project and attempt to build a website on your own. For many authors that will be true, and you may decide to hire a designer to work with you – more on that in a moment – but my point is that *you don't have to*. Here's a case in point: one of the most successful author websites in recent history is StephenieMeyer.com, the official site of the author of the massive international bestselling Twilight Series. Her site uses a very simple template that won't win any design awards. What she did so successfully is update her blog constantly – daily, when it launched – with content that engaged and inspired her fans, and she invited them to interact with her, which made them feel that they were part of this special place in their favorite author's universe. (More about this, as it relates to your website content strategy, in Chapter Three.) The fact that her readers were so satisfied by the content meant that they linked their fan sites to StephenieMeyer.com, and as a result generated enormous traffic.

We've all heard that story about the self-published author who sold books out of her station wagon and then, months or years later, sold the book to a commercial publisher and went on to enjoy significant success. Those self-published authors did it themselves, without a Harvard-educated editor and an award-winning designer. So you see, in our business – the world of books and publishing – there are many happy stories about writers who did it themselves. Those writers might not have thought, when they first put pen to paper, that they'd end up being effective publishers, marketers and salesmen of their own work. But they learned otherwise, *by doing.*

You can do this on the web as well. And just as you might look for a real publisher once your self-published book gets some traction, you can completely re-design, overhaul and re-launch your website with professionals later on. But meantime you can get started on your own, learn a tremendous amount, and start building up that all-important list of email addresses and data about the sources, interests and behavior of your visitors and fans.

Another point about design: you already have at least one graphic handy: your book cover. [Self-publishing sites like Lulu.com offer services to create covers for authors, so if you're going the self-publishing route and don't have – and don't want to –create your own cover it's easy to get help.] Maybe you have a decent photo of yourself as well. Or maybe you have a friend or a kid who can take a picture of you that you can use on your site. Editing photos has become relatively easy to do, and most computer operating systems come with free photo software editing programs included. There are also many trusted photo sources on the web that provide free editing software, like Kodak's EasyShare, or Google's Picasa. Wordpress has a photo editor built in to its content management system, so after you upload your photo you can tweak the size and dimensions right there, in the editing Dashboard.

So you may already have enough to get started. But if you need or want help, there are excellent freelance designers and programmers everywhere, and if you don't have the resources to hire someone to do the entire project for you, you can engage a freelancer for a reasonable fee to help you with specific aspects of your project. One good way to find someone who's right for you is to check the footer (the very bottom section) of a few websites you like, and see if the designer gets a credit. If so, there's probably a link to his or her website, or an email address. So reach out and ask for help. If you find a design you love but there's no credit, send an email to the webmaster and ask for the designer's name, or request that they pass your message along to the designer if they don't wish to share an email address. (When I'm doing research or simply hunting for ideas I often consult the section on the Webby Awards website that lists all the winners and runners-up for their many awards. This is a great way to discover popular and high-trafficked websites, and while many of them were built by big, fancy, interactive agencies, a great many are blogs or sites that started small and grew. You can also consult the Resources section of this book or the companion website, TheAuthorOnline.com, which include a few good places where you can find freelance designers and programmers.)

The more specific you can be with a designer or programmer about what you're looking for, the better. For example: you might want to say you have a small budget and need help with stock photo research, or re-sizing a few images to fit the template you're using. You might ask a programmer to set up your template and hosting plan, and consult with you whenever you hit a wall and need help. You might ask a designer to look at your content outline and help you select the right template, then make some modifications and help you find the right image(s) to fulfill your plan.

Of course it's important that your website looks good, but Stephenie Meyer proves that it doesn't have to be professionally designed and programmed in order to be successful. What it does need is some focused thinking and planning, which is what this manual is designed to help you do. So even if you're working with a designer or programmer the overall approach outlined here will be helpful to you, because very few designers and programmers think like editors or authors, and you inhabit a world of writing and "content." The issues and questions raised here will help you to outline and articulate your goals to them much more clearly.

There's a third scenario that's worth touching on because it brings up the question of project management and how you can apply the skills that professional managers like myself use as they build websites. The author in this scenario wants to do something innovative and exciting on the web. Maybe she has a strong backlist that's spread across several publishers. She want to control everything she does online, and bring it all under one tent. And she has the resources to put together a team of designer/programmer and undertake this project professionally and aggressively.

Hiring professionals is, for most authors, a luxury, and there are great and obvious benefits. But the truth is that these authors will face all of the same questions about defining and articulating who they want to be online and how best to fulfill their vision. If they don't, their website won't fulfill their goals and the experience of building it will be terribly frustrating. So the advice and exercises that come later in this book will be as useful to people who are working with a team as it will be to those who are working alone. Whatever scenario you find yourself in I want to suggest this approach to building a website: *get ready to be your own project manager.* It's a mindset you can adopt, a way of organizing and challenging yourself (if you're working alone) or the folks who are helping you. Question yourself constantly: for example: *do I really need video? Am I going to use it creatively and meaningfully? Is it worth the time and energy I'll spend researching and figuring out how to do it well?*

I think asking questions – *constantly* asking questions – is about the best thing you can do in every arena of your life, but particularly when you're building a website.

## Hiring a Firm

An alternative to building it yourself or working with a designer is engaging one of the small companies or industry groups that specialize in author website-building (and hosting) services, such as the Authors Guild Sitebuilder, AuthorsOnTheWeb.com and AuthorBytes.com. These outfits do good work and can take a huge amount off your plate, so it's worth considering. The downside is that, when you look at the galleries of websites they've built, you'll find that they all tend to look rather similar. And you will still be tied to another entity in terms of making changes to your website, even if you have direct access to a content management system (CMS). If the CMS has been developed by the company, chances are it's not being updated as aggressively as one of the open source options like Drupal or Wordpress, and it may not give you the kind of flexibility you need. And the company may have its own proprietary (or licensed) traffic reporting system that isn't nearly as rich and detailed as Google Analytics, which you can access for free.

So when you're contemplating whether or not to hire an outside firm be sure to weigh the benefits carefully. Yes, they'll do a lot of the grunt work for you, but ultimately what will make your website effective is not so much the gorgeousness of the design but the quality and quantity of the content you have, and the way you present and update it. Only you can ensure that both are consistently – long after the launch, I mean – high. Yes, of course design is important, so be sure, if you're paying a company to help you, that their design work is satisfactory, because the burden of creating and maintaining a high level of content is always going to fall to you, and for your money you should get a design you like and, equally important, a CMS you can easily navigate.

## And Speaking of Content Management...

I can't overstate the importance of the CMS. The most beautiful, classy, elegant web design may win you praise from friends and fellow writers (and even your kid may find it cool, at least the first time he sees it) but if you can't go in there *whenever you want* and easily and quickly add new content and feature new things then you will be completely hamstrung. It's like buying a beautiful yacht that can't be moved from your front lawn to the ocean. All the outfits I recommend in this manual have carefully developed content management systems that are easy to use and intuitive. That means you have the ability to rearrange and add content at will, and keep your website or blog updated as often as you like. In my opinion this is the single most important, and most enabling, development on the web, and it's particularly good news for authors who generate a steady stream of new material and care deeply about how it's presented, edited, updated, edited again, then taken down and replaced with something else.

The main message of this book is that you can get a high quality website-building package that provides customizable templates through an outfit like Sandvox, Wordpress, Square-space, or Blogger and you can build a workable, even a great, site yourself, have full control over it – because of the CMS – and spend a whole lot less money in the bargain. So weigh your options carefully, and be sure you understand what your priorities are before you begin. (Grandma's advice again.)

## What Role Should My Publisher Play?

One final note before we get started. Many authors grapple with the question of whether they should allow their publisher to build a website for them. This is understandably tempting but I advise against it for several reasons beginning with this one: if your publisher creates your website, then he will have the tools and the means to update it. With everything that publishers have to do, and with decreasing staffs and severely taxed publicists and marketing people, the chances that you will have someone's attention for the long haul – e.g. extending beyond a few months after your initial publication – aren't great.

No one knows what's in your heart and mind like you do. And whoever is in charge of your website at your publishing company is just not going to have the time to fully grok what you want to do and how you want to do it, and then commit to your timetable of updates. Most likely they won't be able to turn around on a dime and post changes or updates for you. You wouldn't outsource the updating of your manuscript to someone else – even your publisher – so don't outsource your website either, unless it's to someone who works for you. Your website is your home on the Internet, whether it's a mansion, a condo, a studio apartment, a shack, or just a flagpole blowin' in the wind. Just as you wouldn't want some outside entity controlling how you re-arrange your furniture or decorate your home, you don't want that entity controlling how you present yourself on the web.

If your publisher controls your website he most likely controls your mailing list too. Any large corporation is going to be an absolute stickler for Federal CAN-SPAM laws, which prevent just turning over a mailing list to a third party (and if your publisher owns and operates your website you are, alas, "a third party"). So if you part ways with your publisher, or decide that you can do something much more exciting on the web and want to bring your hard-won subscribers over to your new site, you may hit a wall. I know an author whose publisher, one of the top New York houses, created a simple website for him years ago. Over time it grew out of date, and he hired a team to build a totally new site. Of course his publisher adheres to the letter of the law (as well they should), so when this author wanted to alert everyone on his mailing list (which he had spent many years building) that he had launched a new website (that incidentally would require people to sign up again to continue receiving his email), the publisher not only couldn't turn over the list over to him but they couldn't even do a mailing on his behalf alerting his fans to his new site. This was because the author's new website was no longer one of the company's products, and internal rules prohibited the company from sending emails to its own list about a product that wasn't theirs. So he had to start from square one, at zero subscribers, and slowly build the list again, from the bottom up. Your online fans are an important asset to you, and the Internet – via your website – allows you to communicate with them easily and at very low cost. You need to control how you do that, and you can only do so if you "own" the mailing list.

If your publisher is a publicly traded company or part of a large corporation you'll be limited by what you can do and say on your website, which will be the property of that corporation. The company will have its own rules and expectations, and even your loyal, wonderful editor won't be able to change that. So content may be king, but the king can be dethroned. Better to build your own moat.

And finally: much as you love your current publisher, you may leave him for another. Transferring all the content and other assets from a corporately-controlled website will be bothersome at best and a nightmare at worst.

All that said, there is no reason not to encourage your publisher to include you on its company website, and even to build a dedicated sub-site for you if they offer to. Look at what they're doing for other authors and provide them with all the content they can use: videos, original articles, Q&As, photos, links. Your publisher will most likely be delighted to support your website however he can, for example by providing final text for the sample chapters; cover and interior art if your book has images in it; audio excerpts; advice about which retailers to link to; banner ads for the book, etc. Publishers do get traffic on their websites, and often it's journalists and media people who are looking for new books to include in a theme piece or roundup. Or maybe they're looking for an author with a new book who can be a talking head on a particular subject, or an expert who can comment on a news event or trend. So you definitely want to be there, and you want to give your publisher everything he can possibly use to make your presence as robust and up-to-date as possible. Just be sure that there are links on every page back to your primary site, and that the lion's share of new content originates on your site. Your publisher may be excited about the possibility of promoting you on their site, and they may have good and ambitious ideas. That's great; just don't let them control everything and certainly not the mailing list. Your partnership with them is exceedingly important, particularly in the several months leading up to your publication and the several months following it. Throughout this manual I'll be offering advice about things you can do to promote your work via your website, all of which will be a boon to your publisher. There is much you can do to work with them and and there are ways you can enable them to do more for you. But you need to be smart about how you do it, and you need to assume control.

# CHAPTER TWO

# Getting Started

**If I were an editor** and was sitting down with a nice cup of Lapsang Souchong tea to read your book proposal, I'd be looking for a variety of things, beginning with the most basic: what is this book about? What's this author's point of view, his argument, his story? What sort of voice does he have? By the time I reach the end of your proposal I'd need to know a lot more: Who is this author, what's his background, his track record, his media "platform"? Who's the audience for the book? What are some comparative titles that will help me define the audience to my colleagues and booksellers? How should I package it: What kind of cover should it have? Does it need illustrations? If so, what sort of "look & feel" will best suit the subject and author's sensibility? How would I present it to a sales force? How would I pitch it to a producer at National Public Radio or the "Today Show"? How would I launch this book? What could I do three months after publication? What might develop that would make the paperback, one year later, more commercially appealing? And so on.

All of these are questions that enable a professional reader – an editor or publisher – to "position" or frame a book for all the various constituencies that he needs to address, beginning with his colleagues in an editorial meeting, and then, if he acquires the book for his company, to the marketing people, the sales department, the bookselling community, the media, bloggers, reviewers, social networkers and everyone else who contributes to the beating pulse of our cultural conversation.

That's the path we take in the editorial/publishing process, and it's a good model to use when considering a website as well. So these are the questions I ask when I begin a conversation about what sort of web strategy makes sense for a particular author. I think of an author website as a book proposal writ large and in 3-D. Done well, it contemplates both forest and trees: an author's overall sensibility and the specific works that he has written (and will write).

# The Leading Question

Every time I speak to an author, no matter what the project – whether it's a literary writer or an investment columnist – I begin with those questions that you read in the last chapter and encourage them to think of their website as a natural extension of their work.

So let's start with the basic question you need to address before you can get started:

*What's the overall goal of your website?*

This is a big question so let's break it down into several parts so that you can work through it step by step. This is where you think about what you want (and ardently don't want) to do online, such as:

*Do you want to blog?* If so, will you blog every day, or just in the few months leading up to a new book's publication? Will you run out of steam before the book comes out? Or immediately thereafter? Do you have a subject in mind, both for the launch of your blog and for the first 6 – 12 months of its existence? If you don't, whip out a clean piece of paper or open up a new Word doc and make a plan. You wouldn't just dive in and start writing a book; you'd spend months or even years thinking about it, then you'd write an outline, however detailed. Treat your blogging the same way. Start with a general idea – what's the theme, subject, or argument of this blog? And then make a simple editorial plan: approximately how often will you write entries? What will you do if your main subject goes dormant for awhile but you don't want to break your momentum? Will you have regular features of the blog, things you talk about or post every day/week/month? What do you think the main appeal of your blogging will be? It doesn't have to be earth-shattering; maybe it's as simple as: "my kids will like it." Whatever the reason, just be sure to have one, because it will guide you in those times when your energy falters or you lose your way.

*Do you want to broadcast your thoughts, activities and recommendations, widely across the net by using Twitter, Facebook, and whatever else comes along?* If so, answer the same questions posed above. Then consider: is the goal of your Tweets and Facebook updates to get people to your website so you can introduce them to other aspects of your work, and maybe get them to sign up for your email list so they can get the early word on your next book? Or are these activities just intended to be short bursts you fire off purely for entertainment that don't serve any larger purpose with regard to your website?

*Do you want to open the door to your fans to communicate with you?* And how far do you want to open that door? You could simply display (either prominently or not) your contact information – that would be a conservative approach – or you could build a message board that enables visitors to start their own conversations; that would be ambitious. Or you could let the comments to your blog posts be the main interactive element of your online life. Whatever you do, consider how much of your own time and energy you'll want to devote to this, bearing in mind that it can be a gigantic consumer of both. To say nothing about what it's like to open the door to the opinions of perfect strangers. (More on this in Chapter Three.)

*Or, in a completely different approach, do you want just the bare bones:* your bio; contact info.; a page for each of your books that includes the standard elements like cover art, chapter excerpts, quotes from reviews etc. – e.g. just a basic shack on the turnpike?

*Or: do you want to start simple, then expand slowly and organically,* eventually building your site into something lively and editorially innovative?

*Do you want to use your website to publish new work, test out ideas, share early versions of your books with readers?*

These are the *webixstential* questions you need to wrestle with and answer before you get started. Nowadays, as I've said, building a website or blogging platform is relatively easy and inexpensive. That's the good news, but it puts a burden on you to be smart and focused about what you're going to do, because (the bad news) there are a billion other people out there who are also taking advantage of the many tools that make creating a website so easy. How are you going to build a place that works for you and for your visitors? That's the tricky question that everyone must wrestle with.

## A Few Real-Life Author Scenarios

So here are some real-world examples of authors who have made different kinds of decisions about how they want to represent themselves on the web. These stories will, I hope, help you frame the conversation about your own website. In the Resources section and on TheAuthorOnline.com you'll find a list of author websites that are worth looking at because they represent a much wider range of choices and plans of attack.

One of the most authentic and innovative authors-on-the-web I know is the children's book writer and memoirist Amy Krouse Rosenthal. I edited and published Amy's wonderful memoir *Encyclopedia of an Ordinary Life,* and she's someone who has pushed me, over the years, toward an ever-evolving understanding of what the web can do for an author.

We published *Encyclopedia* in hardcover in January 2005. The website Amy set up was forward-looking at the time because it invited readers to share their own experiences, in the form of "Purple Flower Moments." (I'll let you discover what that means on your own; you have a treat in store.) The physical book itself (on page 167) encouraged readers to share their own Purple Flower Moments, and pointed them to the website, EncyclopediaofanOrdinaryLife.com. So it was a clearly directed process: book to web, driven by the invitation to readers to join the author and create new content that would live in the book's official home on the web.

A book is, of course, a static artifact. Many books get a second life in paperback, but still, the print edition lives on, in pretty much the same form, forever. A website, on the other hand, is a constantly evolving, changing, expanding, environment. So as you think about your website, think about all the ways that it can extend and complement your book(s). Your characters can live on – in a blog, or a diary, for example. You can create maps and timelines, or upload images – particularly color ones that were too expensive to include in the book. And you can invent ways to bring you readers to your website where they can further engage with the content of your book. (Have you noticed that I've done it twice already with TheAuthorOnline.com?)

After *Encyclopedia of an Ordinary Life* came out Amy created another collaborative project called "Lost and Found," in which 150 books were "intentionally left" around three cities (Chicago, Boston, San Francisco). Each book included a letter that invited its new owner to post his or her own story about finding the book on the website. A filmmaker created a video about how Amy's team went about hiding the first batch of books in Chicago, and visitors to the website could watch it and read the many stories that readers posted.

It's a handsome website and it worked very well as a magnet to draw Amy's growing audience of admirers to more content that she and her fans developed around the ideas that her memoir explored. But after a few years it began to feel old, almost stagnant. "Websites seem so last century," she told me at the time. She wanted to do something more immediate, and completely different. So she set up a Wordpress blog called Who is Amy. When I first visited it I was struck by how fresh it seemed. It was the first time I had experienced those little pop-up boxes that appear when you hover over a word, and I was thrilled that I didn't have to click on something that intrigued me and then wait as a whole new page loaded, a process which takes precious milliseconds and some tiny drop of processing power. (This is one of the features I love about Microsoft's new search engine, Bing. When I get horribly stressed out I sometimes imagine that every time I don't have to load a page an angel is getting its wings.) The Wordpress version of Who is Amy is a bit of a miscellany – video here, blogging there, a new book, a radio show, all the previous books she had ever written – but so is life. To my eye her new blog captured the essence of what was going on in Amy-land, a place I have always loved visiting and participating in.

And then, a few years later (towards the end of 2009), the blog too began to feel confining and Amy found herself again wanting to do something new. This time she decided to create….another website. She wanted to get back to basics, and most important to have a landing page – her main home on the Internet – that would clearly articulate the now very diverse multiplicity of the work she had produced since that first website way-back-when. One of her inspirations was the young adult author Jon Scieszka's website, a place that's dense with content but easy to navigate and filled with discoveries. It's also voicey: a visitor gets a distinct and immediate sense of the author's personality, interests and values. And it's well-organized: despite the wealth of content and the many sections on the site you never feel lost, even when you click over to a totally different Jon Scieskzka site, GuysRead.com. One single sensibility – and voice – ties everything together. Amy's new website, WhoIsAmy.com, launched in February 2010 and you can check it out for yourself.

At the other end of spectrum is Dave Kinney, a newspaper journalist who wrote his first book about the annual fishing Derby on Martha's Vineyard. Unlike Amy or Jon Scieszka he didn't have a vast and diverse backlist of titles, and he's not the kind of writer who will produce a book every year, and therefore build up a backlist very quickly. He had written a terrific book, *The Big One: An Island, an Obsession, and the Furious Pursuit of a Great Fish*, it was coming out in six months, and he knew he needed a website to support *that* book. Dave had great photos and knew he'd get a lot more when the book came out and a new Derby began (it takes place every September), and he knew he needed a place where he could write about events as they unfolded and update and add stuff himself, whenever he wanted to. So he worked with a designer to create a simple but elegant website at DavidKinney.net where he could put everything on display and, most important, where people could easily find him – and the extra content he had amassed – if they heard or read about his book.

There are other scenarios, of course. Many authors who have written several books come to feel, at a certain point, "that it's just about time I had a decent website." Perhaps they've published a few books that have done respectably well, but a big one is coming out soon and they know it will get marketing support and media attention. They want to create a place where everyone who hears about the new book can discover a great deal more about the author's previous books as well as other work and interests that may not relate to his books at all.

Another example: columnists and bloggers at news organizations who already have a big audience of readers but know that these days no one can count on staying at the same outfit forever. Even just the simplest website that explains who they are, their areas of interest, resources they recommend, and so on, gives them a way to drop anchor on the web and collect email addresses of people who stop by to find out more about a journalist they admire. If the journalist leaves his current job – and the big platform it provides – he won't completely lose touch with his readers and fans because he'll still have that all-important mailing list and traffic data.

So a website serves many purposes, and much of the preliminary work you must do involves thinking about and identifying what goal(s) your website will serve, both in the near-term and in the middle distance. (Forget about "the future": You should assume that within a couple of years it's likely you'll want to completely reinvent your site and start over, so don't entrap yourself by regarding this as a static project that has to be perfect when it launches. Just try to get it right for now, and give yourself room to grow.)

Whatever situation you find yourself in, I now deem you ready to get started. So here are a few exercises to begin the process.

## The Getting Started Exercises

EXERCISE ONE: CREATE USER SCENARIOS

Whip out a clean sheet of paper (or open up a new Word doc) and write down these questions.

*Who is your audience?*

You probably know a fair bit about the people who read your books if you're an author who has published before. But even if you're a first-time author you probably wrote a proposal when you sold your book to a publisher in which you talked about who the audience is for your book: what other books might they have read (comp titles)? What media (print, online, broadcast) do they consume? What age range are they? What blogs and websites do they visit?

Now start making a list of likely visitors to your website, and think about what might be motivating them to come. I'll give you an example. The list below is a series of user scenarios I created as my team was preparing the wireframes for JustTheRightBook.com, a premium books-as-gift website that launched in November 2009. It relies on real booksellers to make hand-picked, monthly, selections for customers who provide a bit of information about their recipient. Because this is a retail site the user scenarios won't resonate with most authors, but I think you'll get the idea of the process you should undertake. What we tried to do was analyze the broad array of people who might come to our website and the problem they were looking to us to solve. The website, in principle, had to embrace all these user scenarios – it had to make each of these visitors feel comfortable in the knowledge that we could deliver on the promise of selecting just the right book. (Once the site launched we modified this list and presented it to visitors  as a way of suggesting the many people in their lives who might enjoy our unique gift.)

## JUSTTHERIGHTBOOK.COM USER SCENARIOS

•   Woman in her 20s: wants a unique, classy wedding gift for an old friend

•   A Stockbroker for his brother-in-law. He's very busy but promised his wife he'd take care of buying her brother's birthday gift. All he knows about the fellow is that he likes fishing and thrillers

- A Grandmother for her 10-year old grandson. He likes Lego, sports, and computer games. She wants to encourage him to read more

- Aunt for her 8-year old nephew who lives 3,000 miles away, on the other coast. She doesn't see him often and wants to be in closer touch

- Gay uncle for his 13-year old niece. He doesn't have children and doesn't know how to select an appropriate book, but his niece loves to read and he wants to encourage her

- Sales manager for his top client

- Woman in her 40s for her best friend from high school

- Woman in her 50s for her best friend who was just diagnosed with a chronic illness

- Woman for her sister who's an avid reader and goes through at least one book a week. She may be voracious but she's picky, and likes a very particular sort of literary fiction

- Woman for her mother who is recently retired and restless

- Husband for the wife who has everything

- Woman for her grandmother who is in a nursing home

As you create your list of users and user scenarios, remember that Google's innovations in search allow anyone – including you – to be found with just a simple keyword and the click of a mouse. For example: you may be a magician who recently published an article online about magic and cognition, and I might be interested in that subject. If I type "magic + cognition" into Google I just might find your article (or a link to someone who blogged or Tweeted about it), and that would lead me to your website. So there I am, a person interested in your subject: you got me. What are you going to offer me when I arrive? I'll find the link to your article about magic and cognition, but your goal is to get me to do more: to surf around the website and make other discoveries, and eventually to sign up for your newsletter or email alerts so I can find out whenever you publish a new book or article. So the way you label your website – the way you name the sections and highlight the content – is very important. If magic and cognition is a big subject in your field and you find that lots of people are finding you because of that article, you might want to quickly throw up a link that says "More on Magic & Cognition."

But meantime, there's another visitor who found you because he was reading a blog post about your article that compared it with the BBC television show "Jonathan Creek." Visitor #2 loves that TV show and had been searching Google for articles about it. He doesn't care a whit about cognition, and just like the other guy he followed the link and arrived at your website. Now you have two people with different points of view who have come to your site because they were interested in a subject where you are an expert. The home page of your website has to speak to both of them (and the many others who will come for yet different reasons), which means not so much that you should try to curry favor with one sort of visitor or another; instead, you should make the navigation so clear and easy to grok that just about anyone who comes to your website will find a point of entry for themselves. If they love to read books about magic they might immediately click on the Books tab. A young kid looking for a magic trick to impress his girlfriend might click on a link that promises videos of really cool tricks. Maybe you have so many different tricks that you organize them by category, with catchy names that make it easier for a visitor to browse and find the ones that are right for him (Tricks for Kids; Tricks for Hot Dates; etc.) Maybe you happen to be pretty telegenic yourself, so you've set up your Flip video camera and made a series of videos of you demonstrating the tricks. That would be another section, but instead of just calling it "Videos" you could come up with something more enticing, more voicey: "The 10 Most Impressive After Dinner Magic Tricks." (Also consider mentioning in your book that certain videos of complex tricks are available on your website, either in a relevant chapter or on the flap or back cover.)

Now keep making your list. For example: if you have a publicist who's promoting your book, she may succeed in persuading a radio or TV producer to have a look at a video clip of a previous interview you've given, because she's trying to prove how clever and articulate you are. That producer is *really* busy; make it easy for her to find your clips and then discover other relevant and important information about you. And just as you would advise a college student not to be a total goofball on his Facebook page and post embarrassing photos (because content on the web *never dies*) be professional, even as you are being true to yourself. You've made your user scenarios and now you know who might be coming; be prepared for *everyone*.

Maybe you do a lot of lectures to colleges or business groups, and possibly this is something that's important to you – an area of your career that you want to grow. So make that section easy for people to find: label it "Speaking Events & Topics," or something super clear. And when people click on that page reward them: offer a list of your top subjects, with a sentence or two articulating your approach and distinct point of view. If you have audio or video, make the clips easy to find and write a short description of their contents so that people don't have to actually launch them before knowing what they contain. Always try to save your visitors time; make it fast and easy for them to get what they came for. Some lecture agencies – like the Leigh Bureau – produce a nicely-designed brochure for each of their clients that can be downloaded as a PDF. The brochure includes a photo, bio, highlights of the speaker's topics or findings, credentials, contact information, topic categories, etc. If you don't have a professional lecture agent you could still create something similar for yourself using Microsoft Word and a PDF writer like Adobe Acrobat.

Perhaps a lot of your fans are kids or young adults, and perhaps some schools have adopted your book for classroom use. So a bunch of kids are writing homework assignments about your work. How can you help them? Some ideas: a reading guide in Q&A form; images that they can easily download and embed in their paper to help them illustrate a point; a list of books and authors that were important to you as a young person. One author I know has a huge school-aged audience and on her website she reproduced an email that she got from a young student who asked her the same questions that many kids pose. She wrote a long, thoughtful reply, and now it's available to anyone who visits the author's website.

In the old days – the late '90s, early aughts – we talked about "cool features" on websites. The idea was to dazzle and amaze. Nowadays, with so many websites out there – and so many great ones – I believe the bar has been set both lower and higher. *Lower* in the sense that you don't need a fancy programmer to outfit your site with all kinds of technical bells & whistles. *Higher* in the sense that your content must carry the load. (See earlier: *Content is king; long live the king!*). Clearly labeled navigation, created with all those potential visitors in mind, will make the difference between a long, satisfying visit and a bounce. I can't emphasize enough the importance of getting into the head of your visitor. Who is he? Why did he come? What is he looking for? And how can you get him there in three clicks or less?

## EXERCISE TWO: PRIORITIZE YOUR CONTENT

On the home page of your website, what are the three links you want your visitor to click?

When my brother was a kid he loved jelly donuts. He used to look up, as soon as he was a bite or two into one, and announce, his chin covered in powdered sugar: "hey, I'm getting to the jelly!" This became a metaphor in our family for getting to the heart of something. Decades later I'd find myself deep in conversation with my father about something important – love, career, whatever – and as soon as I'd make a trenchant observation he'd perk up and say "ah, now you're getting to the jelly."

So what's central to you? What's the most important content you have? What about you and your work are most satisfying, defining, entertaining, elucidating?

Make a list, and put a check mark or an asterisk next to the most important stuff to make it easy to prioritize later on. If you publish both fiction and non-fiction, perhaps you want to divide things up that way, rather than having one section called Books. But maybe the differences aren't so material – maybe all of your work, in whatever format, is concerned with the same issues and themes. Maybe it would feel forced to split them up, or maybe it would be better to divide them by category (Romance, Mystery, Thriller) or sub-category (Football, Fishing, Curling). What would your reader think? When you look at the list of user scenarios, what do think will work best for the majority of your visitors? If you're finding it hard to figure out what will work best for you, make a list of authors who are similar to you, either in the types of books they write or because they happen to share something in common with you, such as writing across categories (fiction/non-fiction; adult/young adult) or under different names (like Nora Roberts/J.D. Robb). The list of author websites in the Resources section may come in handy for this purpose: to enable you to see how different authors answered that question for themselves and to allow you to compare solutions.

Maybe you have a very busy schedule and you travel at least once a week to do public events. So then your calendar is very important and should be front-and-center, because it's likely that your fans know that you travel a lot. The first thing they might be thinking when they Google you, or come to your website is: I want to know if Joe Author is coming to Pittsburgh soon. (By the way, if this is true for you make sure that you're taking advantage of sites like BookTour.com and Eventful.com, as well as more obvious tools like Facebook and Twitter to alert fans to events and appearances you're making.) One thing to bear in mind about calendars: be sure that they only display current and future events. Nothing is so lackluster as a web page with old, out-of-date, information on it.

## EXERCISE THREE: WHAT DO YOU WANT FROM YOUR VISITORS?

The answer to this question may be "nothing," and that's fine. But think about it carefully first. Understanding what you want from them will help you to frame your hierarchy of content. If you want to hear from your fans, make it easy for them to contact you: create a tab in your navigation called CONTACT, or otherwise prominently place the link that enables them to email you.

One of the most important things you will accomplish with your website is creating a mailing list of people who are interested in you and who care about your work. This list will grow over time, and enable you to send out email blasts alerting fans about a new book, article, media event, bookstore signing, whatever. In other words: you get to control the message that you send out to your fans. So if you're building a website you are almost certainly interested in building a mailing list.

If you want visitors to sign up for your mailing list, create an incentive for them beyond just hearing from you. For example: use your home page to let fans know that you'll be emailing the first chapter of your next book one month before publication, and anyone who signs up for the email list will automatically receive it. Or perhaps you're a self-help writer and you've crafted a special quiz that pertains to your upcoming book (or a backlist title, no matter): let readers know that subscribers to your email alert will get the new quiz – and whatever other features you develop in the future – automatically. Or: announce on your website (and in an email alert) that you'll be giving the first 10 people who reply to you a free, signed, copy of your new book, a chance to join a special webcast, tickets to an event you're appearing at, or the chance to vote on your next book cover. All of these have proven to be effective magnets that draw readers to the websites of their favorite authors.

Once you've identified who will be visiting your website, what they'll be looking for, and what you want to get from them, you'll be ready to start seriously thinking about what sort of content you should present. The next chapter will give you some insight into what features tend to work well on author websites, and will offer guidance for how to think about your own, unique, home on the web.

# CHAPTER THREE

# Thinking About Content

**Now that you've completed the exercises** in Chapter Two it's time for the fun part: to think about content. But before you do, there are two important things to bear in mind.

First: building a website is not like building a house in one crucial sense: if you create a room in your home and then decide it really wasn't necessary – and is too expensive to heat anyway – you can't just hit the delete button and make it go away. Or perhaps you painted it pink and then decided you wanted it green; re-painting will be expensive and time-consuming, presuming you can find a good painter and he actually shows up. With a website, particularly one created on a flexible platform like Sandvox, Wordpress or Blogger, it's quite easy to move your "rooms" around and change the way they look. So at this stage don't get too hot-and-bothered about whether or not to include a particular section on your site, or how it should look or be presented. First assess what you have, and figure out what you need. Once you start actually sketching out or wireframing your site a lot of these decisions will be much easier to make.

Second: You are building v1.0 of YourAuthorSite.com. Websites evolve over time, and the beauty of these new flexible platforms is that developers are constantly coming out with new plug-ins or widgets that allow you to add functionality and display content in new ways. If you don't like the way the content is presented, you can re-arrange it, or delete whole sections and replace them with new ones. So let's get started with v1.0, but as you do, whip out another blank piece of paper/new Word doc and start another list: Future Features. Anything that seems too complex, expensive, premature, *whatever,* stick it on that list. I sometimes create that document in multiple parts, like this:

#### FUTURE FEATURES LIST

- Miscellaneous Future Ideas
- For Version 2.0
- For the distant future
- Major Future Refinements/Additions to Contemplate
- Features I Like From Other Sites

This may sound contradictory, but I urge you to think small and big at the same time. As you surf around the web and examine other people's websites – be they authors or musicians, artists, bloggers, businesspeople, athletes, movie stars – take note of features you like and add them to your list. Be sure to always include a link, because something you describe in shorthand in list form is likely to be confusing to you months later and the link will get you there quickly. [TIP: if you're working in Word the shortcut to adding a link is Command + K on a Mac and Ctrl + K on a PC. First highlight and copy the name of website, hold down the two simultaneously, and paste the copied text into the box that says "link." If you start actively keeping track of websites you'll find this an invaluable shortcut. Note that this is the aforementioned single piece of technical instruction that appears in this book.] There's also a great cloud-based application you can get for free at Evernote. com that lets you actually paste notes to web pages.

Here's an example that's on my list:

*Newsletter options: see CrazySexyLife.com,* the blog of Kris Carr. She offers multiple options for receiving her emails: daily (no longer available), weekly ("the weekly tune-up"), and monthly ("the monthly muse"). The sign-up box is very prominent and nicely designed. By giving frequency options she makes it easy to say yes to "monthly," particularly because one assumes that there must be a ton of people who follow her and subscribe to her emails because she offers a weekly version as well. So it *must* be good.

# What Readers Want From Author Websites: The Codex Group Study

The book business is famous for being an industry that's driven by gut instinct rather than data. There are many reasons for this, some good some bad, but it's a truism that is, well, true. Nielsen Bookscan changed that to some degree when it began to track and report bookstore sales. Now publishers, agents and reporters have the ability to do real competitive analysis on domestic sales of individual book titles. But the business is still far, far away from the more sophisticated, advertising-driven industries that collect and analyze consumer data so they can improve and better position their products.

There is, however, an excellent study of author websites that I have found to be very insightful and useful. It was conducted in June 2008 by The Codex Group, a New York-based company that performs book audience research and pre-publication book testing. For its Author Website Impact Study Codex analyzed data from a highly statistically-significant sample of more than 20,900 frequent book buyers from across the United States, including men and women of all ages, all education levels, and most importantly, all book reading tastes. The survey presented more than 50 categories to its subjects ranging from Literary Fiction, Thrillers and Romance (in fiction), and History, Biography, Diet and Self-Help (in non-fiction). The study found that author websites in aggregate were visited by 7.5% of book shoppers who were surveyed, a greater percentage than is reached by the *Wall Street Journal's* website (WSJ.com), and comparable to the *New York Times'* (NYTimes.com). The survey also found that book shoppers who visited a favorite author's website in the past week purchased 38% more books, and from a wider range of retailers, in the prior month than those who didn't visit an author website.

Peter Hildick-Smith, Codex's CEO and a publishing veteran himself, said of the study: "This was the single largest survey of book shoppers Codex has ever fielded, and probably one of the largest studies of its kind in book publishing. It gave us a tremendous depth of insight into what really moves and inspires book readers in their all-important relationship with the authors they love to read."

These are some of the general conclusions of study, reprinted here with permission from Codex Group:

- 38% of those surveyed said that they had visited an author's website in the past two months

- Less than half as many (17%) said they had visited the author's page on the publisher's website

- 12% signed up to receive the author's email alerts or newsletter

- 2% participated in an online chat or blog about the author

- More women visited author websites then men

- Most (77%) enjoyed reading both fiction and nonfiction, while smaller groups were loyal to just one or the other (non fiction only: 14%, fiction only. 9%)

- Fiction only readers had the highest percentage of website visitors in the past week (13%) and non-fiction had the lowest (3%)

- Regular email bulletins are strongly linked to higher audience participation

The Codex study also identified a list of 25 features that readers look for, and ranked them according to what readers want and would return for regularly. Hildick-Smith told me: "It's very important to remember that a key goal of any author website is to create an ongoing engagement with readers and sustain their interest and reward their loyalty until the author's next new book comes out. A website that has nothing more to offer a fan after just one visit isn't helping the reader or its author."

Here is that essential list of sustaining website elements, organized by ranking with #1 being the most popular and #25 the least. This list combines results from both men and women and focuses on authors who primarily write fiction:

# What Readers Want and Would Return for Regularly to Their Favorite Authors' Websites: Fiction

1. Exclusive unpublished writings by author (deleted scenes, lost chapters, early works, etc.)

2. Schedule of author tours, signings and appearances in your area

3. Author's current favorite authors and recommended books

4. Explainers: inside information on book background, locations, themes, details

5. Download Extras: sample chapters, screensavers, chat icons, etc.

6. Weekly email news bulletin: updates on tours, reviews, next book in progress

7. Contests: monthly games, quizzes, puzzles, chance to win autographed book copies

8. Latest book reviews and news coverage on author

9. Author Blog / Diary: ongoing new entries

10. Links to other writings by author (newspaper, magazine articles, movie scripts, etc.)

11. Behind The Scenes: exclusive insights into the writing life and working author's process

12. Video Book Trailers: for author's current and up-coming books

13. Author Chat: weekly live online Q&A chats with author

14. Author's current favorite websites to browse

15. Author Assist: help author get answers to book research and other questions

16. Buy Direct: purchase author's books, related items direct to support author's site

17. Audios / Videos of author speaking, reading, recent interviews

18. Message Board / Forum: for site visitors to share ideas, recommendations, etc.

19. Biographical information about author

20. Reading Guides and other Reading Group materials

21. Photo gallery of author and locations/people/etc. related to their writing

22. Book jacket gallery including all international editions

23. Author's current favorite music, movies

24. Reading Group Support: sign up for author visits, phone meetings, author feedback

25. Author's Friends: create your own author's friends page, link to others on authors site

The data showed some interesting differences between what men and women look for in a fiction author's website, which Hildick-Smith also analyzed. For example:

• Men rate the "Author Blog/Diary" higher than women do: #3 overall, and 35% return regularly for this feature. Women rank it #9, and 29% return regularly.

• Women rate contests higher: #5, with 34% returning regularly vs. #13 and 22% for men.

• Men rate Explainers at #1 and women rate it #4, but in each case 36% say they return regularly for that information.

• For women, the #1 feature is exclusive unpublished writings by the author (deleted scenes, lost chapters, early work, etc.).

• For men, links to other writings by the author (newspaper, magazine articles, movie scripts, etc.) ranks higher (#6) than it does for women (#11), but one thing is clear: all readers are looking for more writing by the authors they like, whether it's published or unpublished, exclusive or not.

• Women rate latest book reviews and news coverage of the author at #8, and men rate it #5.

I found several surprises here. Both men and women rate Reading Group Guides low (20 for men, 23 for women) but it's worth pointing out that these guides are widely available on publisher websites and author-dedicated sites like ReadingGroupGuides.com. Also, only about 1 in 10 (12%) of book shoppers are active reading group members. Still, my advice is that you shouldn't underestimate the importance of those guides to fans, and if you have one, be sure to include it on your site. And if you don't, consider writing one or finding a smart young person and hiring them to do it. Enabling reading groups to have richer, more substantive discussions about your books is a great thing to do, and will only aid in the good word-of-mouth about your work.

Another thing that surprised me: Biographical information about the author ranks low across the board: 18 for women and 19 for men, but that's because after you've read the bio once, it's unlikely to lure you back for a second read. However: before you edit down your About section, or get lazy about beefing it up, bear in mind that any kid who is writing a paper about one of your books may rely on the information you present about yourself. Many authors have their work featured in course adoptions or as supplementary reading, both at the high school and college level. If you're one of those lucky writers, make sure that your About The Author section is well-crafted, thoughtful, and rewarding to the reader. Even if your books aren't used in the classroom, you should take that advice, because ultimately you want everyone (kids, fans, journalists, media producers, organizations booking speakers) to use the information you present instead of (or at least in addition to) other sources like Wikipedia.

And speaking of young people: Codex's Fiction study found that book shoppers under 35 are particularly interested in exclusive writing, contests and other books and writers that the author recommends.

## What Readers Want and Would Return for Regularly to Their Favorite Authors' Websites: Non-Fiction

The non-fiction results of Codex's survey differ from the Fiction data in several ways. The most striking difference is that non-fiction website visitors report more interest in hearing from the author via regular email blasts and tour updates, and they rank "Links to other writings" third in importance, whereas the Fiction group rates it tenth. For women, Unpublished Writing has the strongest appeal on non-fiction author sites; "Explainers" have the strongest appeal to men.

Here's the non-fiction list:

1. Schedule of author tours, signings and appearances in your area

2. Weekly email news bulletin: updates on tours, reviews, next book in progress

3. Links to other writings by author (newspaper, magazine articles, movie scripts, etc.)

4. Download Extras: sample chapters, screensavers, chat icons, etc.

5. Exclusive unpublished writings by author (deleted scenes, lost chapters, early works, etc.)

6. Latest book reviews and news coverage on author

7. Author Blog/Diary: ongoing new entries

8. Explainers: inside information on book background, locations, themes, details

9. Behind the Scenes: exclusive insights into the writing life and process of a working author

10. Contents: monthly games, quizzes, puzzles, with the prize being an autographed copy

11. Author's current favorite writers and recommended books

12. Author Chat: weekly live online Q&A chats with author

13. Photo gallery of author and locations/people/etc. related to his or her writing

14. Biographical information about the author

15. Audios/Videos of author speaking, reading, giving recent interviews

16. Message Board/Forum: for site visitors to share ideas, recommendations, etc.

17. Author Assist: provide a way for fans to help the author get answers to book research and other questions

18. Buy Direct: purchase author's books and related items in support of author's website

19. Author's current favorite websites to browse

20. Reading Guides and other Reading Group materials

21. Video Book Trailers: for author's current and upcoming books

22. Reading Group Support: sign up for author visits, phone meetings, author feedback

23. Book jacket gallery, including all international editions

24. Author's current favorite music, movies

25. Author's Friends: create your own author's friends page and link to others on author's site

The Codex Group study is an extremely valuable tool to any author who is contemplating a website, whether you're young or not-so-young, specialize in fiction or non-fiction, write for adults, young adults, or children, and are building it yourself or working with a professional designer. Yes, it's a few years old, but in Codex's most recent bimonthly audience study, completed in April 2010, book shoppers were asked how they supported their favorite authors in the past month and the results speak persuasively to the continued and growing importance of author websites: those surveyed said they visited favorite author websites four times more than those author's Facebook pages and ten times more than following a favorite author on Twitter. The list of 25 features that visitors care about is an important checklist you should study and consult for your own website project. I advise you to go down the list and consider each feature, and as you do, consult the list of User Scenarios that you created in Chapter One. Match up the users with the features and see what comes out on top. That will help you create your own hierarchy of features for your site.

I asked Hildick-Smith to summarize the results of his surveys, and this is what he said: "Readers love their authors for very specific, often quite different reasons. They love a novelist for a great read (not what they had for breakfast) and want more of the same kind of great reads, whether from that same author or that author's own favorite writers. Nonfiction readers may be more interested in the author as a personality (and less for their prose), and may want more access to their lifestyle and events. Or they may simply want to learn more from their favorite author about the topics they're best known for, whether in book form or in other media. An author website is one of the very best ways that an author can begin to understand what his audience wants, and to strengthen the relationship between reader and author."

Go to the company's website [http://codexgroup.net/] for more information about Codex Group and the work they do in support of authors.

## Make a Content Plan

So now that we have a useful list of features that we know readers like, and some good, reliable data that helps us weigh how important they are, let's move on to perhaps the most pressing questions:

- What stuff should I put on my website?

- How often must I update it?

- What do I do about Facebook and Twitter (and whatever else comes along afterwards…)

- Must I include a message board?

- And finally: how do I get started. Literally.

Pull out the list of User Scenarios you created in Chapter Two and keep it handy. Then take out yet another clean sheet of paper/open up a fresh doc and make a list of everything you have. It might look something like the list below, which is a hybrid of features I've assembled from my research into author websites and my own work building them. I've allowed the list to get so long in order to make a point: that you should be comprehensive in your early fishing expeditions. When you make your list, go ahead and include the kitchen sink. (Or, to be true to the fishing metaphor, the whole can of worms.) You can (and must) go back and prioritize it, and pare it down. But for the moment give yourself free rein. As you review my list, cross off the things that strike you as ill-suited to you and your work. That exercise may further help you to position and define yourself, because sometimes articulating who you are not is a fine way to get to the heart of who you are. So yes, some of these items will seem silly or irrelevant, but in rejecting them you will be defining what sort of content best suits and represents you. It may also give you some ideas that you wouldn't have had otherwise.

And now here's the list.

## The Long List of Author Website Content

• Sign up to receive email alerts/newsletters, including an incentive to the visitor to provide her email address.

• A short description of each book.

• A sample chapter from each book.

• The cover of each book and a selection of interior images.

• Media updates, reviews and videos of TV interviews about a just-published book.

• The Introduction by a well-known expert that appeared in one of your books.

• The original book proposal you submitted to your agent and/or to publishers, perhaps with some notes by you about how the book evolved and changed after that initial description and outline.

• Quotes from reviews and blurbs from other writers.

• Video book trailer(s).

• Conversations: write a Q&A that addresses all the questions you are likely to get from the range of visitors you identified in your list of User Scenarios.

• Articles you've written for magazines, blogs, regional newspapers, etc. If you're not allowed to reprint the articles, either on a web page or in a downloadable PDF, include a link. [Remember to periodically check all the links on your website to make sure they haven't broken or been removed by the originating website.] Include a short summary or description of the piece – as little as a sentence (as Malcolm Gladwell does on his site) or a paragraph or two – and, if relevant, some thoughts about why it was important to you or your career. Remember that people can probably find your article on the website of the entity you wrote it for by using a search engine. On your website you have the opportunity to offer a bit more about every feature and piece of content you include. So if it's relevant and interesting include some additional commentary or reflections. Many visitors will be coming for precisely that insight, which they won't find anywhere else.

• Another thought: take a look at CNN.com to see how they annotate their articles. A recent piece by the journalist Gayle Tzemach Lemmon is about women in Afghanistan under the Taliban. CNN added, in the left column, "Story Highlights," which summarizes the most important points of the article. A busy person would find this very reader-friendly. So if you have a lot of articles or essays, especially long ones, it's a feature to keep in mind. Like most news websites CNN also includes links to "Related Topics."

Here's a website that's trying – in as clean and clear a way as possible – to help the reader "get to the jelly," as my brother would say.

• Your early work: if you're a journalist or writer who has published extensively, consider including the first article you wrote, or offer a sampling of your early work. If you have a lot of work stretching across many years, find an appropriate way to organize it: by decade, category or theme, for example.

• Videos of you in television interviews or giving a lecture. [Note that YouTube allows you to easily embed a video directly onto your website. If you have lots of videos you should consider setting up your own YouTube Channel, which you can customize with your own design so it echoes your website. This way you can benefit from the huge number of people who are surfing and searching on YouTube. com, and you can provide a simple way for people to publicly comment on and recommend your videos.]

• Audio clips of you in radio interviews.

• AudioBook excerpt.

• Book-related archival material: if you wrote a book long ago, some visitors may be interested to see the original press release that your publicist wrote, or an ad that the publisher ran in a newspaper. Or the original hardcover jacket art and flap copy. Or a sample page spread.

• Unpublished writings: deleted scenes or chapters; an alternate ending; a new epilogue or introduction; photos or other elements that ended up on the cutting room floor.

• A gallery of your international book covers, including a link to each foreign publisher's website. [Note: it's tempting to link directly to the product page of a publisher or retail site but bear in mind that these links often tend to be unstable and when they break they generate an error message. Test them frequently to be sure they're still working.]

• If you lecture: a list of topics you talk about, with a line or two explaining each, and a list of the most important places at which you've spoken. Be sure to convey the range: small companies; local reading groups; charitable organizations; large corporations; colleges & universities; chambers of commerce; press associations, etc. Include the contact information to make it easy for organizations to reach you about a speaking engagement.

• Create a press kit that includes downloadable photos, in black & white and color, in hi-res and low-res, along with credit information, so that media outlets can easily find and use the photos you want them to. If you have a publicist, ask for advice and find out if the publisher is preparing any materials you might be able to use to good effect on your site.

• A Reading Group Guide.

- A "Readers' Guide" aimed at young readers who might be writing a book report about you or your work. Think of it as a "Cliffs Notes" of your work, and address the major themes/issues/ideas you cover; talk about the process you went through in researching your subject, the authors and books that inspired you, etc.

- A Teacher's / Educator's guide, if your work is commonly used in classrooms.

- Quizzes, Tests & Polls. These are easy to include in websites because developers have created widgets and plug-ins that enable you to make these features interactive, and they are very popular, particularly quizzes.

- Authors you admire and/or who influenced you. Think about including more than just a link to their books on Amazon or IndieBound: if there was a great interview with them in the *New York Times,* a smart review in an academic publication or a terrific interview with Jon Stewart on the "The Daily Show," include those links as well.

- Culture and Pop Culture that you consume and recommend: books, music, films, websites, blogs, articles, smartphone apps, people to follow on Twitter, restaurants, etc.

- News in Your Field: if you're an expert in a particular field your readers may be interested in new research, articles, blog posts, books, essays, reviews, controversial news interviews, etc. that have caught your interest. If you feature such information regularly it will be an incentive for your readers to come back to your site frequently, or to subscribe in an RSS reader.

• Biography: a detailed biography of yourself. You can use this space to provide whatever facts about your life and career you wish to include, and also talk about things that may interest your readers: what other writers (and artists, businesspeople, politicians, etc.) influenced you and why/ how. If you've had a long and complicated career, consider creating an FAQ about yourself. Be sure to link your Conversations/Q&As to your Bio page.

• Current Projects: could be a part of Bio or could be a separate page within your Bio/About section. Here you can promote upcoming works, let your fans know what's coming soon, and include your email sign-up box so they can be alerted to news or new works being published.

• Film adaptations: information about movies, plays, or any other sort of adaptation of your work (even if it's a funny YouTube video that your kid made). If your work is featured on IMDb, Amazon, Netflix, link there as well.

• Photographs of yourself. Readers love to see informal photos of their favorite authors that go beyond the traditional book jacket illustration. Pictures of your office, or the space where you work, will be of particular interest, as will places that are important to you and your work.

• Calendar. Only include a calendar if a) you have a decent number of public events and b) you are committed to keeping it up-to-date. You can include lots of events: media appearances, public lectures and speaking engagements, book signings, publication date, etc. You can also include other fixed dates like the anniversary of the publication of your first book, births/deaths of well-known people who influenced you (with quotations if you have room), etc.

• Buy the Book: links to purchase. Be sure to include several alternatives, including IndieBound.com, the site that helps people find and do business with independent retailers. Your "buy" links are more than just a convenience to visitors (because virtually everyone in the world knows how and where to buy a book these days): they say something about you. If you have a broad representation, including your favorite national retailer and your favorite local retailer, your fans will see that you care about *all* outlets that sell books, and that you offer your support broadly to the retailers who support authors. Many people prefer to support local retailers rather than chains or behemoths, so I recommend you always include them. And if your work is available overseas don't limit yourself just to retailers in the USA; include at least one online retailer in each country where your work is available. Also: if you make your books available at a special discount for educational or other purposes like corporate sales or premiums be sure to say so and clearly state how best to contact you.

• Quotes that inspire you: there are widgets or plug-ins available that will let you feature a quotation and attribution, and you can set things up so every time a visitor refreshes his browser a new quote appears.

• Reader feedback: what your fans say about your work and / or your website.

• Twitter and Facebook widgets: if you're active on Twitter and Facebook you can embed their update widgets on the home page of your website so that your visitors can see all your recent activity without having to leave your site.

• Blog: you don't have to limit yourself to just one blog; if you're feeling very ambitious you can feature multiple blogs and cover more than one subject.

• Maps, walking tours, photos, essays that convey the flavor of local history and locations in your book.

• Explanatory features like a timeline of events, a character list or a family tree or chart showing how the people in your book are related. There are several cool technologies you can use on your website to create timelines (TimeToast.com) or organize your photos into a narrative that lets you connect people, places and time (MemoryMiner.com).

• Color photographs that you had to print in black & white in your book.

• How to contact you. Before you activate your contact links think about the potential impact of getting a high volume of email. Many authors include detailed FAQs on their sites, which they continually expand as questions and comments come in from visitors. This is a good way to take the burden off yourself to reply to lots of email. Another thing to consider is the issue of spam. If you include your actual email address – JoeAuthor@aol.com – you open the door to all kinds of spam bots. This is why most authors include an email form, rather than an actual address, on their websites. If you don't want to do that, another solution is to disguise your address so it's not readable by a machine, for example: JoeAuthorATaolDOTCOM. But that doesn't look very pretty and some people who aren't terribly web-savvy may be confused by it.

• A Message Board. Later on this chapter I discuss the pros and cons of message boards, so read on.

## The Schedule of New Content

So you've made your list, and you've pared it down. Now you're faced with the question: how often must I add new material to my website?

I think the simplest way to answer that question is by reminding you not to over-promise. If you provide a conspicuous place on your website for constantly updating material – like a tabbed box that rotates content (see TheDailyBeast.com for one of a million examples) – then you are implying that new stuff will continually appear in that space. Those boxes cry out: "hey, there's so much happening in my life/world/career that I need a rotating box to organize just the newest, most topical material!" If you have the desire and the personal bandwidth to constantly update your website then that's great, and you'll find many templates to accommodate you. You'll also satisfy many hungry fans who will return to your website on a regular basis to get new material. You'll also encourage them to sign up to receive your email alerts because, knowing that you frequently update and add to your site, they're not going to want to miss anything.

But it's possible that what you need is simply a relatively static, elegant, home on the Internet that can contain everything that's important to your work (and no more) and allows you the flexibility to easily update it yourself whenever the need or desire arises.

As you think about the home page of your site, and as you look at website templates, consider the burden that design places on content. If you don't have a lot of content to launch with, don't choose a template that has four columns; try to find a good one that has just one or two. You can always expand later. As you look at the templates, contemplate how your content will fit in the various layouts. As you think about that you'll be forced to focus on the question of how often you will be updating your website. Now consult the editorial plan or roadmap you made that outlines the sort of content you'll include and how often you'll replace it with new material.

## Getting Organized: Make a Sketch

Before you start looking at templates and making real decisions about how your website will be organized it's a good idea to sketch out the elements on a piece of paper. This is a great way to focus your mind on the hierarchy of content and the experience of the visitors who will come to your site.

The first thing a good designer will do is create a wire-frame, basically a blueprint of a website. In tabs and boxes the wireframe outlines where the main content elements will go: how many columns will there be? What content goes in each? What are the most important elements to feature on the home page? How many main sections (tabs) will there be? What are the names of each section? What text links must persist on every page? How is video featured? Is there one page for all videos or do they appear on many (or all) pages on the website?

Your wireframe is like a visual Table of Contents.

Making a wireframe forces you to think through the process that a visitor will make: he arrives at the home page, looks at a featured piece of content, clicks and is taken…. where? Everything that's clickable has to go somewhere logical. So think like a user (referring again to your User Scenarios) and plot his course, and make sure that every time he clicks he's taken somewhere of value to him. The fewer the clicks the better. Think about your website, just for a moment, like a supermarket. A well-organized store is clearly labeled and you don't have to push your cart from aisle-to-aisle to find what you're looking for: you have a basic understanding of where the different products are and how they are grouped together. A good website works the same way because the folks who designed it did so with the user in mind. They wanted that person to "get to the jelly," as my brother would say, in as few clicks as possible. A visitor's value to you isn't the amount time he spends on the site, it's the positive experience he has. Because with websites, as with supermarkets, you want the visitor to be satisfied and return. So make it easy for him.

Don't worry about making it "cool" or "fun" or otherwise experiential; focus instead on delivering great content in whatever form you wish in as few clicks as possible.

So sit down with a blank sheet of paper, a pencil and a large eraser (this time don't work on your machine, do it the old-fashioned way) and start to channel that user. (Staples, by the way, sells an oversized graph pad that's 11 x 17 and is perfect for sketching out web pages.) Visit lots of other author websites and click around. As you do, think about what the author intended you to experience and discover. Was it clear? Did you have to click many times to find the best stuff, or the thing you were looking for? Was it cluttered and disorganized? Do you see a way that she could have simplified it?

If you like working on your machine there are some free or inexpensive products you can use to make charts, including Microsoft Word, which lets you create shapes – large and small boxes – that very nicely represent tabs and areas of featured text and images. There's an inexpensive diagramming program I've used and like a lot at LovelyCharts.com You can try it for free and see if it works for you. They enable you to create various kinds of charts including wireframes (you can also make flowcharts, sitemaps and network diagrams, and they have a very good video tutorial that teaches you all the basics). There's also a program I discovered while it was still in the beta phase (and free) at GoMockingbird.com which allows you to create "wireframes on the fly." It's very easy to use and is a great way to organize yourself in a dynamic, hands-on way.

# Take a Look at Templates and Other Websites

Now, with your User Scenarios and the first draft of your Content List in hand, it's time to start checking out the actual architecture that's available to you. In the Resources section you'll find links to free Wordpress and Google Blogger themes, as well as to Sandvox, the Author's Guild website building program and other resources. If you're working with a designer this is still a good exercise and I encourage you to look both at templates – because they are empty of real content and therefore quite easy to imagine your own material there – and at many other websites that are devoted to an individual and his or her work. This will help you to see how other people have worked through the challenges of how to present themselves and their work on the web, and may give you some useful models to discuss with your own designer.

Another good way to communicate your aesthetic sense to a designer is to show her some magazines and book covers you like. I know a designer who always asks new clients to give her a list of 5 - 10 websites, magazines and book covers they like, and to provide short notes about why – not just "it's pretty" or "it's elegant" but to get useful feedback like: "I like the font; I like the use of white space; I love the presence of video on every page; I like the way the navigation reads – it's very simple and easy to find your way around; I like that it's spare and clean, without too much going on; I like that there's tons of content and it's clearly a site to get lost in; I like that the author's personality comes out so strongly; I like that it's understated and a bit mysterious;" etc. You get the idea….

## Blogs and Social Networking

The most frequent question I get from authors is: *should I Twitter?*

Blogs are still ubiquitous and people start them every day. I did so myself, in August 2009, to indulge my obsession with New York City's new elevated park, The High Line. [You'll find it at LivinTheHighline.com in case you're interested.] But the cultural tide has turned, for the moment anyway, to micro-blogging platforms like Twitter and Facebook.

The answer to the question "should I blog" is almost easy. Since blogs are a relatively long form (compared to the new micro platforms) you only need to ask yourself the obvious questions: do you have something to say, day after day? Do you love your subject so much that you'll be energized to write about it continually? Is it a subject that people care about? And: do you have a plan for spreading the word about it, because a blog in a vacuum doesn't do anyone any good, unless there's something you are so obsessed about that you just have to get it off your chest every few days.

The answer to the Twitter question is basically the same. The best advice I can give you is to make a plan. But here's something to remember and carefully consider as you think about microblogging. You're a writer, and whether you write fiction or non-fiction you are at heart a storyteller. So you have the opportunity to use Twitter as a way to construct a narrative of sorts. You don't have to; it may be enough to toss out your daily ruminations or provide a running commentary on what you did or ate or read during the course of a day. But consider something more meaningful: creating an unfolding story that evolves over the course of many Tweets. Maybe you want to experiment with actually writing a short piece of fiction and distributing it in the spirit of Charles Dickens: serially, but using the technology of day. Or perhaps you're engaged in a fundraising project and every day you Tweet an update about funds that were raised and stories about the people who contributed. Or maybe you're involved with an organization like Habitat For Humanity, and you're building a house for a family in your community. You could Tweet a construction update every day, including videos of people hammering and putting up walls, and comments from your fellow builders.

Each Tweet or Facebook status update can be a brick in that building. When the reader clicks on your links she comes to your website where she can watch a video or read more of the story – several paragraphs or pages, depending on how much you have to say. And while she's there she can also make discoveries about other aspects of your work, and maybe read a chapter from your last book. Then the next day she'll see you Tweeting again, and so on.

The pipes that carry Internet messages are clogged to bursting with useless Tweets and information. That said, millions of people are using Twitter, Facebook, MySpace, Google Buzz, and everything else that comes along to vacuum up information about the things and people they care about. So if you're an author and you care about reaching and building your audience, should you Tweet? Well, yes, if you have something to Tweet about. If you don't, my advice is to spend some time thinking about how you can do it in an innovative way that's true to you and the work you do. Brainstorm, and make a plan. And then, once you've figured it out, incorporate Twitter into your website, either by posting a widget that displays recent Tweets and allows readers to scroll through them, or just via a simple, old-fashioned link: *Follow me on Twitter.* But start with the idea, and let it drive everything. Eventually, if it's a good idea, it will develop a life of its own, and you will discover ways to nurture it on your website. And one thing I've learned over the years, both from my early experience as a publicist and my later experience on the web: one idea leads to another. What's exhilarating about working on the web is that all the ideas you have – whether they are good (and successful) or bad (and abject failures) – are your own form of R&D because you can test them out and analyze the results (see Chapter Four). And then do it better next time.

## Message Boards and Letting the Crowd In

And finally, message boards.

What thinking process should you go through in order to answer the question: *should I include one?*

Here's a question back atcha: do you want to communicate with your fans?

No is a fine answer, and there are many reasons to decline. You're a writer, not necessarily a public figure who wants to engage with fans and strangers. Maybe you honestly don't care what other people have to say about you, your work, your ideas, your subject. Or maybe you just feel there aren't enough hours in the day to keep up with what may end up being a steady stream of "feedback": questions, comments, criticisms, self-indulgent sharing, etc. And it's true that once you open the door to people they come to expect that you are listening and paying attention to them. If you don't reply you risk disappointing or, worse, irritating people who will not necessarily hold back their feelings.

My advice, if the answer isn't immediately clear to you, is that you think carefully about what your goals are for having a public message board. There are many good ones, which gets to the other side of that question: why you would want to create a space for your fans to interact with you and with each other. Many writers are hungry for feedback from their fans: they want to know what people thought of characters or stories or entire books. They are intrigued by the suggestions people make, or touched by the stories they share. Here is a golden opportunity for a writer who spends many hours indoors, staring at a computer screen, to interact with a universe of individuals who are connected to him through his work and his interests. There is as much to learn and receive – to embrace – from these folks as there is to run away from in horror. Some authors actually use the Acknowledgments section of their books to thank readers and visitors to their website for urging them to return to a particular character, or to alert them to errors they find. For these authors a website is a way to open the door to readers and let them into their world.

Creating a place where readers can interact with you, an author they care about, is a huge incentive to them to keep visiting your website. And while they are there, chances are they'll sign up for your email list, and find out when your new book is coming out. They may pre-order it, and tell their friends about it, on Twitter perhaps or by linking to your site on their Facebook page. That one act, of allowing users to connect with you and with other fans who feel connected to you, can be a powerful way to build loyalty and to get feedback that may have some value to you. And if you are lucky, the community will grow and prosper on its own, with minimal participation by you. But there are millions of ways for people to connect with each other on the Internet. If you are going to provide one more, on your personal website, you should do so with a reason and with a plan. So make another list and consider the ways in which you feel a public message board will be beneficial to you and what role you intend to play on it. Are you, for example, going to respond individually to people who post comments or start conversations – are you going to engage with them in a personal, conversational, way? Or are you going to use it purely as a way to make announcements about events in your career or your life? It's important to think this through before you take that message board live and be consistent, so you don't create false expectations.

And do so with your eyes wide open. There's a dark side to message boards: snark – and often worse: meanness, rudeness, vulgarity – abides. These wretched excesses are enabled by the ease with which people can assume anonymity on the web. I don't know if there are statistics about this, but my sense is that the overwhelming majority of people who post comments on message boards and blogs do so under an assumed name. Most people don't have the desire to be obnoxious; they want to share their opinions and comments but they don't want to be recognizable for whatever reason. Many other people, however, go to the web precisely because they *do* want to rant and attack. More than once I've had to help a client who has a message board deal with this situation: someone makes a post, another person attacks it in a very crude and thoughtless way, and a third person steps in and says "hey, this is our place and we're all abiding by the golden rule: Be nice or get out." Then the snarky one really goes on the attack and things escalate. Big websites with staffs are able to monitor comments and remove the nasty exchanges, and all good message boards are to some degree self-policing. But you're an author and this is your home on the Internet, and no one wants a loud, creepy, angry person shouting at the other guests in his house. So that's another consideration to keep in mind as you decide how much of the outside community you want to let in.

Nowadays, as blogging has become so popular and accessible, most people who venture onto the web do so by creating a blog. And the whole point of a blog is that it's a two-way street: you post, readers comment. There are many vocal purists who insist that if you're going to start a blog you absolutely *must* enable the comments. Otherwise, they ask, why bother?

I say balderdash. Many people are using blogging software to create a space for themselves online – because it's easy, it's free, it's adaptable – but they have no interest at all in hearing back from total strangers. It's your choice, and you can build your site without enabling comments and then add them later.

A simple way you can acknowledge the presence of your fans on a blogging platform is to include a "tag cloud," a visual representation of the most popular articles on the site, which is a convention of blogging. When you post an article or content entry (anything from your author bio to the description of a book) you tag articles by subject or theme. In the tag cloud the ones that are clicked on the most appear in a larger font. For an example see the O'Reilly Radar blog. In the right column there's a tag cloud called "Radar Topics." And on "Schott's Vocab," Ben Schott's perfectly delightful blog on the *New York Times,* there's a "Vocab Cloud" (you have to scroll all the way down to see it). Including a tag cloud is a way to invite the crowd in (and acknowledge its presence) without giving them the keys to the kingdom.

But it may be that the answer for you isn't a blog or a message board at all; perhaps Twitter or Facebook are simpler, less time-consuming ways to engage. As you consider that, remember that the difference between Twitter and Facebook is that Facebook is a more private, enclosed community where you interact with your "friends" (some of whom you may not even know, of course) and your groups. (Note that if you want to open up your Facebook presence to the world at large you need to create an official fan page, not a group that's associated with your personal profile. Fan pages are publicly accessible by anyone – and therefore more useful as a promotional platform for you and your work; personal pages and groups are not.) Twitter, on the other hand, is the whole world in bites of 140 characters: a loud, busy, open space with a constant stream of news, ideas, links, notions, reviews, comments – everything, including massive amounts of purely useless blather. So once again: think carefully about your own work and about who you are comfortable being on the web, and develop a game plan for yourself. And remember that you can always expand your reach as you get your sea legs – you can start slowly and ease into it.

# CHAPTER FOUR

# The Joy of Data

**Once you get your website built** the first thing you must do – on the day it goes live, *no exceptions!* – is create your Google Analytics account.

As a book author you are accustomed to having precious little, if any, information about your readers. Until the introduction of Nielsen Bookscan in January 2001, the publishing industry flew virtually blind in terms of data about how many books were sold and where. But the information Bookscan provides (which authors can't access anyway, because the licenses are too expensive for any individual to purchase) is pretty thin: it's broken down by account, can be sorted by date range, and includes some geographic data. But it remains inaccessible to authors and is an extremely blunt instrument compared to a tool like Google Analytics.

## Mining and Using Your Data

What Analytics does – for free, with virtually no effort required from you (all you have to do is drop a few lines of HTML code onto your website) – is provide a rich trove of data that will give you invaluable information about your visitors: where they are coming from, what pages they visit, how much time they spend on each page (so you can tell if they are actually reading or just browsing), and where they go. You can determine the most trafficked pages, both for entry and exit. And you can sort by date range, selecting just a single day or a longer period spanning weeks, months, or the entire life of your site. This enables you to see if something you did – a media appearance, a review, the publication of an article you wrote – attracted visitors to your website and if so, where they went and what they read. You can see how many unique visitors you've had (again by day or date range) and which pages they looked at during the time period you selected.

Another valuable metric is the "bounce rate." When someone "bounces" off your website it means they arrived and immediately left without reading or clicking on anything. A high bounce rate might suggest that you're not doing a very good job of engaging people who come to your site, and you need to find better ways of communicating what your content is on the home page. Having an accessible, easy-to-use content management system (CMS) allows you to tweak your copy and presentation, and then check back, day after day, week after week, to analyze your traffic data and see if your changes are having an effect.

You can also click on a map of any country in the world and find out how many visitors that country sent. Even better: you can drilldown to individual cities in each country. As I mentioned earlier, this makes it easy for an author to plot a book tour because he can know what regions send him the most traffic, and therefore where he has the most recognition and might sell the most books. It would also give an author a better understanding of what his international traffic is. And you can sort all the metrics Google makes available by date range, which means that for any piece of content on your site you can see how many people from which countries or cities read a particular article and how much time they spend reading it. (Even if you don't get a lot of traffic Google Analytics delivers. My blog got very few visitors in the first couple of months, but I could always tell that my mother was reading it because the village where she lives showed up in the city search. Thanks, mom!)

It's such a rich program that you will explore around for months before you'll fully grok all that's available to you. But it is blissfully simple to get started and Google provides excellent and comprehensive Help documents to answer your questions and teach you how to get the most out of the program.

Here's a real-world story to give you a sense of why Analytics can be so valuable to authors. I have a client who writes regularly for her own website and many large news/culture sites. After we launched her website I was combing through Analytics to see what the numbers could tell me about our traffic, and I noticed something interesting in the Content Drilldown, the list of pages that are viewed by visitors. I sorted the content by the order of unique visitors and saw that the 19th most popular article had the highest "Average Time on Page," which meant that even though it wasn't the most popular piece on the site it was the one that visitors spent the most time on: they were clearly reading it, not just landing on the page, quickly browsing it, and moving on. It was an article about how to improve the quality and quantity of your sleep. So I called up the author and said "you know, people are really liking your article on sleep. You should write another one." So she did, but before we published it we pitched it to a highly trafficked women's website. We were able to tell the editor of that site that our own analytics told us that this author – a well-known writer whose website gets a high volume of monthly traffic – was hitting a sweet spot in her audience with the subject of how to sleep better. The first website published the piece, and it was then picked up by an even bigger website. Both of those sources sent tons of traffic to the author's own site, where we also posted the article.

That one little metric in a sea of data – a majority of people like this author's advice on the subject of sleep – gave us a clue that had great value to the author.

Another example: I have a client who runs a lot of quizzes and assessment tests on her website. Google Analytics confirmed what we assumed would be the case when we launched the site: people *love* interactive quizzes. So we came up with a plan to add new quizzes on a monthly basis and to feature them on the home page as soon as we posted them.

Note that there are other affordable analytics programs available, including Mint, which at the time of writing cost just $30 for a site license. Do some research and find the one that works best for you.

## Buying & Selling Ads – Yourself

So you can see how knowing what your readers are looking for and responding to can guide you as you make decisions about what to feature on your home page. That, in turn, will better engage your readers and lower your bounce rate. You can also use that information to help you market your website with a Google AdWords campaign if you choose to. AdWords is a program that lets you bid on keywords that users on the Internet might click as they are searching for something. The paid ads are the ones that appear on the right side of a Google search results page or at the top, highlighted to separate them from the real, user-driven results. The way the program works is you select keywords (Google has a tool that makes this very simple) and then you decide the maximum amount of money you're willing to pay if someone clicks on your ad. It's a bidding system, so if, for example, my author had wanted to run a campaign in which she identified keywords like "sleep," and "Improve your sleep," she might set a maximum bid of $1.50 per keyword and an overall daily maximum spend of $100. That way she can control how much she spends – if the campaign is very successful and lots of people click on her ad, she doesn't run the risk of spending way beyond her budget. But she can adjust it the next day and increase the amount of money she's willing to pay and the daily budget. And she can change the keywords and the ad copy at will, then track the results (because Google lets you associate your AdWords and Analytics accounts) to see which combinations performed best. She can continue to tweak and track her ads – buying new keywords, writing new ad copy – until she gets the results she's looking for. Then she can start all over again with new combinations. Google Analytics also allows you to create Goals, so if you're selling something – a book, for example – you can establish that clicking on the link to buy the book is a Goal, and then easily track how often that Goal was fulfilled and which keywords drove your success. *The New York Times* recently launched a similar program that allows inviduals and small companies to build and manage their own ad campaigns on NYTimes.com.

Another program Google has is AdSense, which opens the door to other individuals and merchants who might want to place ads on your website. You won't get rich from this kind of advertising (and many find it intrusive and even a bit tacky) but it costs you nothing and could bring in a few dollars.

There are many good books about marketing websites (I've listed some in the Resources section) and the subject is way beyond the scope of this book. But the tools for advertising and promoting your website are easy to use and you can do a lot for very little money. The process is similar in spirit to what I've outlined in this manual about building a website:

you can start small and simple, then grow and expand as you collect information and see how your efforts are working. The beauty of the web is that you can test and analyze results based on a rich, almost endless stream of data that you may harness. And you don't need a degree from the London School of Economics to do it.

## Closing My Browser Window

I promised to be brief in this book. The goal was never to be comprehensive, and so I trust I've left you with some questions. Good. The answers are out there, so take a deep breath and don't be intimidated. Count on making mistakes and having a few freak-out moments. Go slow, just as you did when you began your first book. Have a good time.

And don't get so absorbed that you forget to walk the dog.

*Click.*

# My Bookmarks

Here is a collection of websites and companies that provide a variety of useful services. I've used most of them myself, though not all (but the ones I haven't used come highly recommended by people I trust or are from organizations I know to be reliable). This list is constantly updated on TheAuthorOnline.com and you will find all the links there. So visit the Resources section if you want to click through directly.

## Author's Guild website builder: *Outsource Your Website*

The Author's Guild is a great organization that lobbies in support of authors on every  front. They have a toolkit for building websites and also offer hosting plans.

## Blurb.com: *Print-on-Demand and Self-Published e-Books*

Long gone are the days when people in the publishing business used to sniff at "vanity presses." Today self-publishing is an honorable route, and there are many options available, including Lulu.com and Amazon's Create Space. If you're producing a book with illustrations – photographs or color art – they will give you the best printed quality. Of course you should do your own research and compare companies and websites, to see what feels like the best fit for you and your project.

## CreativeHotlist.com: *Freelance Designers*

A listing of individuals and companies that provide help with a variety of creative services including graphic, web/flash multimedia design, art direction, programming and development.

## DesignRelated.com: *Freelance Designers*

This is a great source of freelance designers that's searchable by tags, so you can find people by location or the area of design they specialize in. The site includes web and graphic designers.

## Dropbox.com: *Storage in the Cloud*

This is one of my favorite programs and I rely it more and more as time goes by. It's on online storage and backup facility that enables you to place files in a folder (a "Dropbox") on your desktop, and then access them from any computer or mobile device. When you add or change a folder on one machine (say you're in Paris, enjoying a lovely vacation and working on your laptop) the file is updated in the cloud, so when you open the document on another machine (your desktop at work or home) it's the new, updated version. Everything is backed up and if you accidentally lose something you can nip that panic attack in the bud because Dropbox has saved and indexed it, and offers several simple ways to find it. And you can share files with other people, so if you are working with a designer, developer or project manager this is a great (and free) way to share files without relying on email.

## Drum Set: *For Your Time Out*

For those moments when you want to tear your hair out, this is a great place to hang out for a bit.

## GoDaddy.com: *Hosting & Domains*

I've used GoDaddy for several simple websites and I'm always grateful for their excellent 24/7 support. They also have good site documentation, but it's so easy to get a customer rep on the phone that I tend to avail myself of that great benefit. But I've heard complaints about GoDaddy from some people, and know that no hosting service will be perfect for everyone. Karelia, the makers of Sandvox, have a good comparison chart on their website to get you started, but there are zillions of hosting services out there and you can – and should – do your own research before you commit to a service. Be sure to carefully consider how much space you really need, and remember that you can always increase your plan as your traffic and the content you are hosting grows. So there's no reason to commit to the most robust, expensive, plan, even if you're feeling really ambitious.

## iStockPhoto.com: *Stock Images*

If you need images for your website this is a great site to know about. They have a massive and ever-growing library of affordable images, and a very good search engine that allows you to refine and narrow your search. If you're working with a designer you can create your own "lightbox" of images, then share it with him or her. Or vice versa. Another photo service I like but haven't used as much is MorgueFile.com. For free images see Wikimedia Commons below.

## LovelyCharts.com: *Software for Site-Mapping, Wireframing, Organizational Charts*

This is a web-based software program that enables you to create sitemaps, wireframes, organizational charts, diagrams and more. They have a very good video tutorial that runs you through all the basics (very quickly) and you can share your charts with your collaborators. It's inexpensive and very easy to use – a great way to organize your thoughts and get them down on paper. Another great site, in beta at the time of writing, is GoMockingbird.com (see below).

## Lynda.com: *Software Training Online*

I love this site. As a do-it-yourselfer (and a DIY evangelist) I find it a liberation. They have tutorials on every software product imaginable, and once you watch some of their videos you'll understand why they're relatively expensive (at the time of writing, $25 per month to access the entire library).

## MailChimp.com: *Email Service Provider*

MailChimp is one of the top (though not the biggest) of the email service providers, or ESPs. There are several good ones (Constant Contact is another) but I like MailChimp because it has a sense of humor and is wonderfully simply to use. You can create a template for your email right there on its website, and they have a rich, easy-to-use metrics program that allows you to gather and compare statistics for all of your email campaigns. They also have great support, both via live chat and site documentation. Karelia, the maker of Sandvox, has a handy chart on its website that compares email service providers. There are others available on the web and you can Google it and do your own research.

## MemoryMiner.com: *Digital Storytelling Application*

This app lets you organize your photos and create a narrative by linking them to each other based on the people, places, and things that appear in them. In the book I write about another cool technology, Timetoast.com, that lets you create timelines on the website.

## Pixlr.com: *Photo Editing Online*

This is a photo-editing website that enables you to edit images online. It's free, so is a great alternative (especially for beginners) to expensive programs like Adobe Photoshop.

## Sandvox: *Simple, Elegant, Software for Building Your Own Website*

Sandvox is made by Karelia Software and works only on a Mac. I've used it myself and love the way it's so intuitive and easy. Karelia has one of the best and most user-friendly Help sections I've encountered on the web, and the download comes with blogging software built-in, along with all of Google's tools you'll need to optimize your site and set up Analytics. If you're planning to build your own website or blog but don't use a Mac, see Squarespace below.

## SaveVid.com: *Software to Upload and Download Large Files*

An easy-to-use web-based program for downloading online videos from sites like YouTube, Google Videos, etc., in multiple formats.

## SendSpace.com: *Software to Upload and Download Large Files*

This is one of many free file uploading services. I've used them before and found the service to be easy and fast.

## Slideshare.net: *Upload and Share Power-Point and Keynote Presentations*

This is a website app that enables you to upload and share presentations using PowerPoint, Keynote, Word and PDF documents. You can add audio to create a webinar. For business book authors or anyone who gives lots of speeches, this is a great way to present your ideas.

## Shelter Build.com: *The Blog of the Shelter Institute*

This blog will inspire anyone who's a do-it-yourselfer at heart. It's for builders who use wood and traditional carpentry tools, not technology and robotic kits like the ones you find in *Make Magazine,* another of my favorite publications. One day I'm going to spend two weeks during the summer taking the barn building class at the Shelter Institute. It's got nothing to do with websites, but I include it here – along with a shout-out to Etsy.com – because it speaks to an impulse so many of us have to create things – to build it ourselves.

## Squarespace.com: *Software for Building Your own Website or Blog*

I haven't used this product myself but someone I trust has and he recommends it highly to non-professionals. Squarespace has its own analytics system and also provides a hosting service. Its website is well-designed and seems very easy to use.

## ThemeForest.net: *One of the Best Sources for Elegant Wordpress Themes*

ThemeForest has a wide range of Wordpress themes and HTML templates. There are scores of sites that offer templates but I've found ThemeForest to be the best and easiest to search. You can browse categories and find templates that were created for specific purposes: portfolios (art, photography), blogs (personal and news/editorial), corporate (business, marketing), retail (fashion, travel, food, etc.), non-profit, entertainment and more.

## Wikimedia Commons: *Database of Free Images*

Wikimedia Commons is a database of freely usable media files, including photographs and videos, to which anyone can contribute. In Spring 2010 the database contained over 6.5 million files. Another large database of images can be found at Google Images.

## Wordpress.org/extend/themes: *A Massive Directory of Free Wordpress Themes*

At the time of writing there were 1,194 free themes in this directory. There's a browse function that lets you filter themes by tag (colors, number of columns, features, subjects, and more).

## Zamzar.com: *File Conversion*

A free, easy-to-use website that does file conversion.

# A Sampling of Author and Book-Specific Websites Worth Looking At

Here is a list of author and book-specific websites for you to look at and compare. Look for updates on TheAuthorOnline.com, where you will find all the links and can click through directly.

AUTHOR SITES:

## LaurellK.Hamilton.org

I don't love this site, but it gets a fair bit of traffic, so clearly she is doing something right for her fans. She also runs a message board, so if you're contemplating that this would be a model worth looking at.

## ChuckPalahniuk.net

This is an interesting site for many reasons: it has tons of stuff to read by a great variety of writers. It's a big tent for Palahniuk's work but also other writers he admires and nurtures. He runs a Writer's Workshop from this website and charges a fee to access it. There, writers can read works by others and get feedback to their own. It's a very busy site in terms of its design (a plus for some, a minus for others) and one you can get lost in. Palahniuk has long been active and smart on the web.

## DavidBaldacci.com

Here's a well-organized site by an author who publishes across a variety of categories and has written many books. He also has a message board.

## Orson Scott Card

The sci-fi writer's website is Hatrack.com. This site was clearly built a long time ago – June 8, 1996, to be exact – but there's a reason that more than 10 million visitors have paid a call: not only is Card an extremely popular writer but he has a great deal of interesting material aimed at all kinds of readers from adults to kids, writers, students, and teachers. The design of his site doesn't enable him to display new content very well, but he writes a weekly column and runs a Writers Workshop.

## Sue Grafton.com

This feels just a tad gimmicky to me, and old-fashioned as well – the home page and some of the interior ones load with flash animation and a soundtrack – but there's a lot of content and it's worth taking a look and seeing how Grafton decided to organize a huge and diverse amount of content. Her message boards, like Baldacci's and Hamilton's, feel like they were built several years ago and are in need of a re-think. Looking at some of these old-fashioned message boards and comparing them to successful blogs is a good exercise if you're contemplating creating a forum for communicating with your fans.

## Atul Gawande

Gawande.com is a simple, very elegant, site built on a Wordpress platform.

## CarlHiaasen.com

Hiaasen writes for kids and adults and has sections for each. He also has a Q&A for each book and one about his movies and his personal life. He has a section I've never seen on a website before called "Friends," where he includes links to websites of his friends and organizations he likes. It's a nice feature. On the home page he's carved out a space to feature a news item – an interview with CBS "60 Minutes" or a review of one of his books, for example.

## Alice Hoffman.com

Hoffman includes podcasts, essays, a blog, and a separate section for her films.

## KhaledHosseini.com

I have a lot of respect for Khaled Hosseini, not only for the quality of his writing but also for the work he does for the Afghan people through his foundation. His website isn't as robust as you might expect from a writer of his stature, but he runs a blog and publishes a very good newsletter every quarter, and past editions can be downloaded from his website. He also has podcasts. The site was built by AuthorBytes.com.

## DebbieMacomber.com

See how Macomber organizes all the different series she writes as well as other features like contests, a knitting club and recipes.

## StephenKing.com

He ain't The King for nothin'. Stephen King has been innovating online for longer than most authors, and he's got several excellent sites. Surf around, just for the fun of it, and see how he does it.

## JKRowling.com

One of the most trafficked author websites on the Internet.

## MichaelConnelly.com

Includes a photo gallery with slideshows depicting the LA he writes about; lots of newspaper articles with titles so you have a sense of what they're about; lots of video and audio links. It has a simple design but there's lots of satisfying content for the fan. Has Related Links in Bio section.

## MalcolmGladwell.com

I like the way that Gladwell breaks down each of his books and explains how they're organized and what each section contains. For most of the books there's a good deal of supplemental material, from the publisher's press release to extended excerpts and Q&As about the books. I also like the Etc. section, which points a visitor to websites of Gladwell's friends and miscellaneous articles and links.

## Michael Pollan.com

A very handsome, newly launched website by the peerless author and journalist.

## StephenieMeyer.com

See Chapter One for some thoughts about this very successful website.

## MicheleJaffe.com

This is a site by an author who writes for teens. Her publisher, HarperTeen, also has a site dedicated to Jaffe's book Bad Kitty (as they do for all their authors). This is a good example of an author whose publisher built a web page for her, but she knew she needed her own (much more personal, distinct) site.

**SOME AUTHOR WEBSITES BUILT
ON THE SANDVOX PLATFORM**

RebeccaChace.com

DonnySeagraves.com

CantRememberWhatIForgot.com

SimonCheshire.com

AlistairForrest.com

BodilMartensson.se

To view a larger gallery of Sandvox websites:
http://www.sandvoxsites.com/

**BOOK SPECIFIC SITES**

## Freakonomics and SuperFreakonomics

I really like Freakonomicsbook.com: it's clean, well-organized, and while much of the content lives on other websites (including the *New York Times,* where the authors have a very popular blog); it feels unified. The FAQ's are a great idea because they give a simple snapshot of the theory behind the books that's fun to read. I also love the design. Note that the designer, BeingWicked.com, gets a credit in the footer, so you can hop over the their website and find some other author sites. Also note that this site was created using Wordpress.

## BrainRules.net

A well-conceived site with lots of information and a straight-forward, very modern design. Note that he links to a blog created using Google's Blogger platform.

## 59Seconds.wordpress.com

This is a very simple Wordpress site devoted to the book *59 Seconds* by Richard Wiseman. It came on my radar because his publisher ran an eye-catching (because it was so elegantly designed) ad on the NYTimes.com, and the click-thru link came to this page. It doesn't have a great deal of content (and it's now quite outdated – clearly this is a site that was built to promote a new book and it's not being tended to now that the main publication effort has passed) but there's a video of the author and an excerpt, and I'm betting it cost very little time or money to create.

## MyUnfinishedBusiness.com

One of the things I admire about this website is the amount of carefully curated content the author, Lee Kravitz, has included. And not only does he make it accessible via a regular page on the site but he also offers visitors the opportunity to download PDFs of his material. It's interactive: Kravitz invites visitors to send him their own ideas and stories that connect to the theme of his book – taking care of unfinished emotional and spiritual business – and his intention is to blog about those stories and share them with his community. It's a great example of an author who got it right.

## TheNightofTheGun.com

This is the site that David Carr, the media columnist for *The New York Times,* launched to promote his memoir, *The Night of the Gun.* It's an all-flash website, so not the kind of thing that any author could create who didn't have a lot of programming experience and a strong background in flash design, but I include it here because it's a very good example of a voicey, content-rich website that's geared to present a massive amount of material that a printed book can't possibly include. Carr is also a very honest and authentic guy with a compelling story and these days, on the Internet, that's a refreshing combination. If you're interested in viewing some other all-flash websites check out JeffersonRabb.com; Jeff has designed a lot of terrific author (and other) websites and his work has been profiled in *The New York Times Book Review.*

# Miscellany

This is a collection of articles and books I've found interesting, helpful and useful. Look for updates in the Miscellany section of TheAuthorOnline.com, where you will also find all the links. Like the resources in the first two appendices, many of the urls are quite long and creating footnotes for them would be unwieldy. The list below gives you a sense of what is available on the website.

## SOME ARTICLES I FOUND INTERESTING OR USEFUL

### *Blogger vs. Wordpress Comparison Chart*

This is a handy chart that outlines and compares all the key features on both Blogger and Wordpress.

### *Google's SEO Starter Guide, Google Webmaster Central Blog*

Available in 40 languages, this is a solid introduction to SEO.

### *How To Use Twitter as a Twool,* by Guy Kawasaki

A smart and insightful piece about Twitter.

### *In the Next Revolution, Atoms Are the New Bits,* by Chris Anderson

A fascinating Wired magazine article about DIY product design and custom manufacturing. It's all about how anyone with an idea for making something can design it himself using free, open source tools on the web and then access manufacturers, both in the US and overseas, who can create and ship the finished product, all at an affordable price.

### *77 Ways to Get Traffic*

A free resource that's been floating around for awhile. It has some good tips and ideas.

## *Should e-Books Be Copy Protected?*, by David Pogue

A fascinating article about *New York Times* tech columnist Pogue's experiment with removing the copy protection from one of his e-books, and the impact it had on sales.

## *Why Twitter Will Endure*, by David Carr

A great piece by the *New York Times* media columnist about how to use Twitter as a tool that enables your interests and brings value.

### SOME GOOD BOOKS

This is not an exhaustive list for sure, but you're at the beginning of this process and there's no reason to overload you.

## *Duct Tape Marketing: The World's Most Practical Small Business Marketing Guide*, by John Jantsch

Aimed at businesses, this book still has lots of good advice for anyone who's trying to promote and publicize a website.

## *Google Analytics, Third Edition,* by Jerri Ledford, Joe Teixeira, Mary E. Tyler

This is a well-written guide to Google Analytics that also has a section or chapter on AdSense and AdWords. It's not cheap – a $35 paperback at the time of this writing – but it's an excellent resource and companion to the wealth of information you'll find on Google's website.

## *Search Engine Optimization: An Hour a Day,* by Jennifer Grappone and Gradiva Couzin

A systematic, easy-to-follow primer on search engine optimization – SEO – one of the most important forms of web marketing.

## *SEO Fast Start,* by Dan Thies

This is a free e-book that covers all the essentials of SEO: mapping out keywords strategies; developing and optimizing web pages; building links; measuring results; and more. The author also runs a blog on the subject.

## *The New Rules of Marketing and PR: How to Use Social Media, Blogs, News Releases, Online Video, and Viral Marketing to Reach Buyers Directly,* 2nd Edition, by David Meerman Scott

This book on modern marketing and public relations on the web comes highly recommended to me, and was a *Business Week* bestseller.

## *Wordpress for Dummies,* by Lisa Sabin-Wilson

Normally I prefer the Idiot's Guides to Dummies, but this is what my local bookstore had when I needed it, and I've found it to be very clear, easy-to-follow, and comprehensive.

# Acknowledgments

I've been blessed over the course of my life and career: I've had many people who encouraged me to venture way outside my comfort zone and learn new things. Even when I tried something and failed these folks egged me on, urging me to try again, but perhaps to do it differently this time, or to start something altogether new. Having their support gave me the courage to develop curiosity and patience, enabled me to periodically reinvent myself, and allowed me to experience the great joy of discovering new things, from the piano to the Internet. I never would have written a book like this without them and I'm grateful for the different gifts they gave me.

Some provided opportunity – and took a flyer on me, without knowing how it would work out. Others were teachers or mentors who offered patience, wisdom, insight, support. All of them understand (or understood, for sadly some of them are no longer with us) the redemptive power of humor in any situation, and perhaps that's the greatest gift, and lesson, of all.

Thanks to: David Black, Rafael Cortes-Colon, Joni Evans, Chip Gibson, Bianca Gray, Kelly Jewett, Susan J. Knox, Jean Fair Mitchell, Marika Moosbrugger, David Rosenthal, Tony Schulte, Steve Ross, Frances Taliaferro, Alberto Vitale, E.K. Weedin, Jr., Barbara Winslow.

Special thanks to three wonderfully talented, smart, patient and gentle people I have worked with on several web projects over the past few years: Hugh Hunter, Lesley Marker, and Jeff Rabb. I learned a great deal from each of them and never once did I hear their eyes rolling as I struggled and bumbled along. Thanks, guys. And to Joan Feeney, for the hours she spent imparting advice that turned out to be invaluable and spot-on every time: a thank-you hardly seems adequate, but it's what I have to offer. I'm also grateful to Antonella Iannarino and Dan Wood for their careful and thoughtful reading of the manuscript of The Author Online and their invaluable suggestions. And I thank the wonderful Daniel Rembert who designed the cover and the interior.

Most of all, though, I got to do what I do and become who I am because of Ann Godoff. That has made me the luckiest girl in the world, and not a day goes by that I don't remember it.

# About the Author

Annik La Farge spent 25 years in the book publishing business, beginning as a publicist. In 1990, when she was associate publicity director at Random House, she launched Random House Large Print, the first industry initiative to publish simultaneous large print editions of major releases. She went on to become vice president and associate publisher at Times Books and Villard – both imprints of Random House – and later Simon & Schuster. In 2001 she moved into a strictly editorial job and became a senior editor at Crown. Her last publishing job was at Bloomsbury USA where she was publishing director.

During those years she was part of the team that oversaw the marketing and publishing plans for every author on the list, and over the course of more than two decades worked with a great many authors including Marcus Buckingham, Jimmy Carter, Mary Higgins Clark, Hillary Clinton, Jackie Collins, Jeffery Deaver, Pete Dexter, E.L. Doctorow, Eve Ensler, George Foreman, Jon Krakauer, Bill McKibben, George

McGovern, James Michener, Ben Schott, Neil Sheehan, Daniel Silva, and Gore Vidal. Among many other duties she was involved in the early efforts to create e-books and develop strategies for digital publishing. As an editor she acquired and edited non-fiction books by Roy Blount, Jr. *(Feet on the Street)*, Max Brooks *(The Zombie Survival Guide)*, Robert Frank *(Richistan)*, Garry Kasparov *(How Chess Imitates Life)*, Nando Parrado *(Miracle in the Andes)*, Mo Rocca *(All The President's Pets)*, *Charles Schwab's New Guide to Financial Independence*, Kara Swisher *(There Must Be a Pony in There Somewhere)*, The Onion, Benjamin Wallace *(The Billionaire's Vinegar)*, and the gentlemen who wrote the classic *I'm a Lebowski, You're a Lebowski*, among many others.

In the late 1990s, at the height of the dot com boom, she took a year away from publishing to join entrepreneur and journalist Steven Brill in the development and launch of Contentville.com, where she published an original series of e-books and oversaw the website's bookstore.

In 2008 Annik left publishing to start her own company, Title TK Projects, which specializes in website project management, editorial work, and consulting on digital strategy. Recent author websites she has project-managed include MitchAlbom.com, FrenchWomenDontGetFat.com, MireilleGuiliano.com and TaraParkerPope.com. She also helped create the book section at wowOwow.com, oversaw the launch of the investment blog JubakPicks.com (a 2009 winner of the SABEW "Best in Business Award"), and the e-commerce site JustTheRightBook.com.

A lifelong New Yorker, Annik lives just above the High Line in Chelsea, and writes the blog LivinTheHighline.com.

www.ingramcontent.com/pod-product-compliance
Lightning Source LLC
Chambersburg PA
CBHW052147070326
40689CB00050B/2424